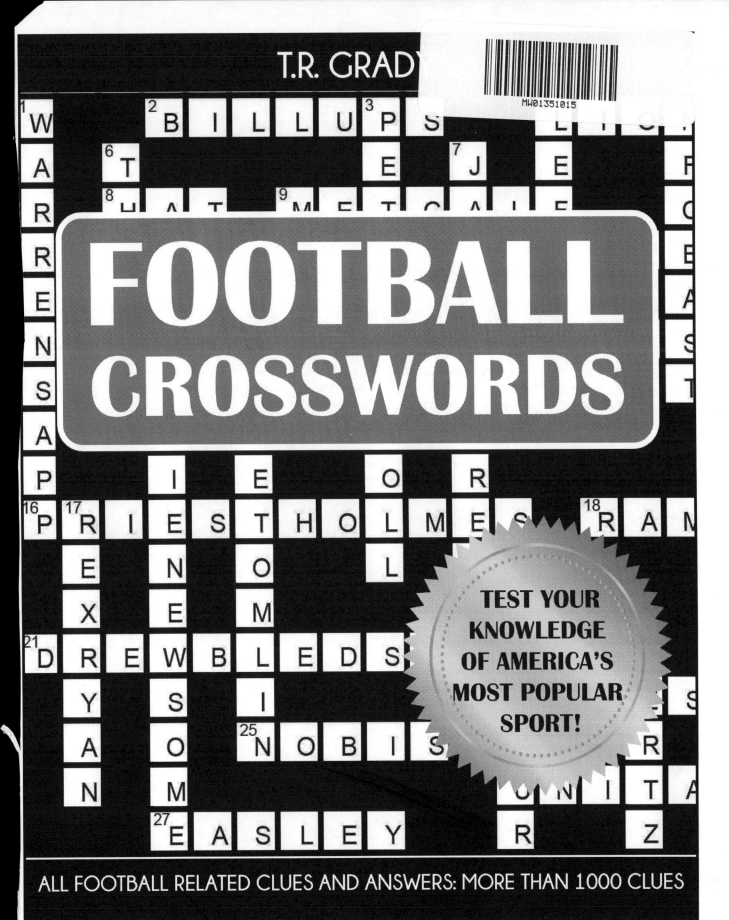

Published by Dylanna Press an imprint of Dylanna Publishing, Inc.
Copyright © 2022 by Dylanna Press

Author: T. R. Grady

All rights reserved. No part of this publication may be reproduced, stored in a retrieval system, or transmitted by any means, including electronic, mechanical, photocopying, or otherwise, without prior written permission of the publisher.

Limit of liability/Disclaimer of Warranty: The Publisher and the author make no representations or warranties with respect to the accuracy or completeness of the contents of this work and specifically disclaim all warranties, including without limitation warranties of fitness for a particular purpose.

Although the publisher has taken all reasonable care in the preparation of this book, we make no warranty about the accuracy or completeness of its content and, to the maximum extent permitted, disclaim all liability arising from its use.

This book is not endorsed by and is not associated with National Football League.

Trademarks: Dylanna Press is a registered trademark of Dylanna Publishing, Inc. and may not be used without written permission.

Puzzle #1

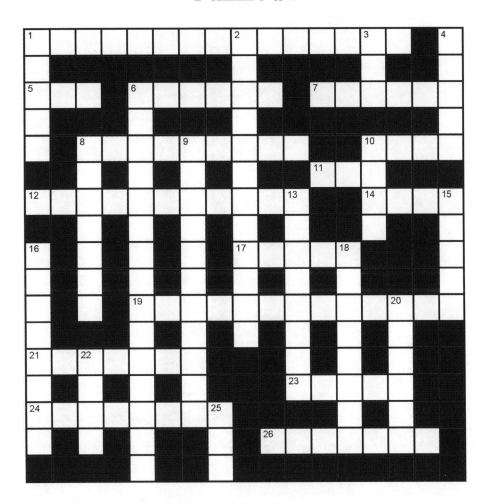

Across

1. CLE (9,6)
5. OJ Simpson college (3)
6. Kansas City (6)
7. K (6)
8. 1976 MVP Baltimore Colts (4,5)
10. Times Peyton won MVP (4)
11. Falcons Super Bowl appearances (3)
12. 1980 Browns team nickname (7,4)
14. Troy Aikman college (4)
17. Bucs WR, Mike (5)
19. Nicknamed "Snacks" (5,8)
21. Determines if there is a penalty or not (7)
23. Michael Vick number (5)
24. 1st Chargers QB to throw for 400 yards in a game, 1980 (3,5)
26. Bengals TE, caught 2 TDs in SB XVI (3,4)

Down

1. Browns RB, Nick (5)
2. DE (9,3)
3. Drew Brees is now an analyst at this network (3)
4. TD receptions J.J. Watt had in 2014 (5)
6. Sings Sunday Night Football song on NBC (6,9)
8. Giants RB, Saquon (7)
9. 1976 DPOY LB PIT (4,7)
10. Bills Super Bowls lost in a row (4)
13. Legion of Boom (8)
15. Seahawks owner, Jody (5)
16. SB XXXVI MVP, NE (3,5)
18. Jimmy Johnson appeared on this reality tv show (8)
20. New Orleans (6)
22. Packers are owned by (4)
25. QBs drafted before Brady (3)

Puzzle #2

Across

1. Direction Norwood kick missed (4,5)
5. _____ formation; formation where offensive team has one running back in backfield with QB (3,4)
9. 1998 MVP DEN (7,5)
10. 49ers DE, Brother Joey (4,4)
13. 2009 DPOY GB (7,7)
16. 1984 MVP MIA (3,6)
17. SB XXIII MVP, 49ers WR (5,4)
19. 1986 MVP NYG (8,6)
20. Times Ray Lewis led the league in tackles (4)
21. 2004 DPOY BAL (2,4)
22. Length of end zone (3,5)

Down

2. Titans RB (7,5)
3. In 1996 the Browns became the (6)
4. The front of the end zone (4,4)
6. A long, distinctly arching pass (4)
7. SB VIII MVP, MIA, Larry (6)
8. Ravens owner, Steve (9)
10. Beat DEN in Super Bowl XXI (3,4,6)
11. SB XLIII MVP, WR PIT (8,6)
12. San Francisco (5-6)
14. 1972 MVP WASH (5,5)
15. 2003 CO-MVP TEN (5,6)
16. Browns career INT leader, FS, Thom (6)
18. Number of players on the field on defense (6)
19. Longtime Bills coach, Marv (4)

Puzzle #3

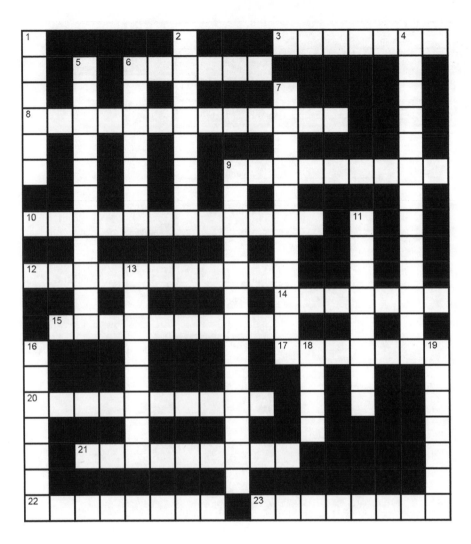

Across

3 Infraction of rule that both teams be on their own side before ball is put into play (7)
6 Cleveland (6)
8 Champ Bailey was traded to Denver for _____ (7,6)
9 Drafted by Jets ahead of Dan Marino (3,6)
10 Colts GM as of 2022 (5,7)
12 QB Tom Brady replaced (4,7)
14 Giants (3,4)
15 Only coach to win championship in the NFL and AFL (4,6)
17 "Too Tall" (2,5)
20 Most INTs in Lions history, longtime Steelers DC (4,6)
21 1995 DPOY BUF (5,4)
22 Weeks in NFL regular season (8)
23 Fired as Giants head coach after 2021 season (3,5)

Down

1 Futbol (6)
2 Giants owner (4,4)
4 A play in which the ball reverses direction twice behind the line of scrimmage (6,7)
5 1st Broncos QB to finish season with 100+ passer rating (5,6)
6 1983 DPOY DE MIA Doug (7)
7 Rams owner (4,7)
9 Falcons OC during Super Bowl collapse (4,9)
11 Chargers Pro Bowl DE, has a brother also in the NFL (4,4)
13 7x Pro Bowl DT, 1st ever Cowboys draft pick, HOF (3,5)
16 The area between the end line and the goal line (3,4)
18 SB XX MVP, CHI, Richard (4)
19 Illegal filming moniker (7)

Puzzle #4

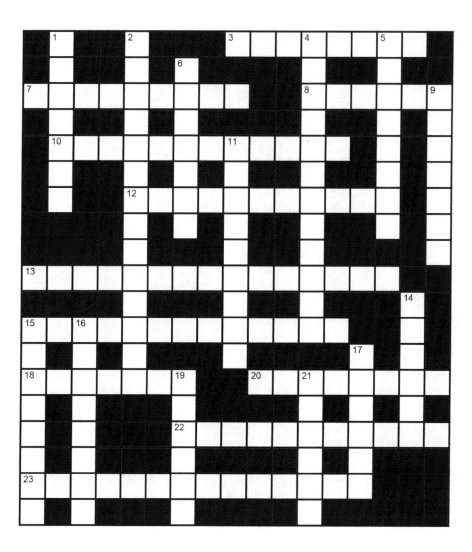

Across

3 Coach nicknamed "Bum" (8)

7 Browns (9)

8 1977 DPOY DE DAL Harvey (6)

10 SB XLV MVP, GB (5,7)

12 1980 DPOY Raiders CB (6,5)

13 Drafted 1st overall in 2007, Raiders (8,7)

15 Players that try to get past the offensive line (9,4)

18 Cardinals division (3,4)

20 New England (8)

22 1961 MVP GB (4,7)

23 Beat CIN in Super Bowl LVI (3,7,4)

Down

1 1989 DPOY MIN Keith (7)

2 Jaguars QB as of 2022 (6,8)

4 2019 MVP BAL (5,7)

5 Terrance Knighton nickname (3,5)

6 Bengals franchise leader in punt return TDS, Lemar (7)

9 Giants division (3,4)

11 SB XLIV MVP, NO (4,5)

14 Broncos WR Courtland (6)

15 Head Coach with most wins ever (3,5)

16 The protective grill that forms part of the football helmet (4,4)

17 New York (6)

19 Panther owner, David (6)

21 Bills 88-99, HOF, Thurman (6)

Puzzle #5

Across

1. Tennessee (6)
2. _____ kick; kicking the ball from where it has been placed on ground or tee (5)
4. Kicker who specializes in punting (6)
7. Miami (8)
11. Bears coach hired in 2022, Matt (8)
12. 1988 DPOY CHI LB (4,10)
14. Beat SF in Super Bowl XLVII (9,6)
16. Baker Mayfield college (8)
17. Ravens HOF safety (2,4)
19. Packers (5,3)
21. First inductee into Texans ring of honor, WR (5,7)
22. Youngest QB to ever start a playoff game, BAL (5,7)

Down

1. Nickname for Aikman, Smith, and Irvin (8)
3. SB XXVIII MVP, DAL RB (5,5)
4. Interception of a pass (4)
5. Yards based on the difference in starting field position between the teams and penalty yardage (6,7)
6. Vikings WR, Justin (9)
8. Nickname for Steelers defense in the 1970s (5,7)
9. 1996 MVP GB (5,5)
10. Saints RB, Alvin (6)
13. SB XXXIV MVP, STL (4,6)
14. Joe Namath nickname (8)
15. Beat DAL in Super Bowl X (8)
18. Cowboys 99 yard TD run in 1983 vs MIN, Tony (7)
20. One player obstructing another player with their body (5)

Puzzle #6

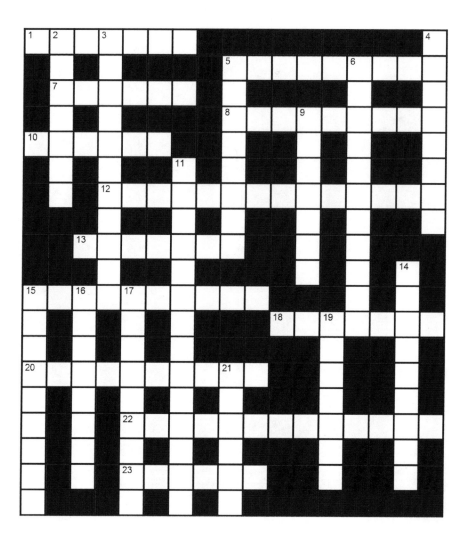

Across

1 Falcons OL, 69-86, Jeff (3,4)
5 Leads Cowboys in career INTS (3,6)
7 Jon Gruden nickname (6)
8 2015 MVP CAR (3,6)
10 SB IX MVP, PIT, Franco (6)
12 LAR (3,7,4)
13 Texans (7)
15 Eagles QB, Oklahoma (5,5)
18 WR Cowboys to Bills, Cole (7)
20 Colts coach 2018-2022 (5,5)
22 OL (9,4)
23 Holds record for longest INT return, BAL (2,4)

Down

2 Jets division (3,4)
3 Region between lines of scrimmage (7,4)
4 Team that gets the ball first in OT is determined by a _____ (4,4)
5 Tom Brady college (8)
6 Won Super Bowl III (3,4,4)
9 Commanders division (3,4)
11 Jets/Giants stadium location (4,10)
14 Yard line where red zone starts (3,6)
15 SB XLVII MVP, BAL (3,6)
16 Colts stadium (5,3)
17 SB LII MVP, PHI (4,5)
19 Chiefs division (3,4)
21 C (6)

Puzzle #7

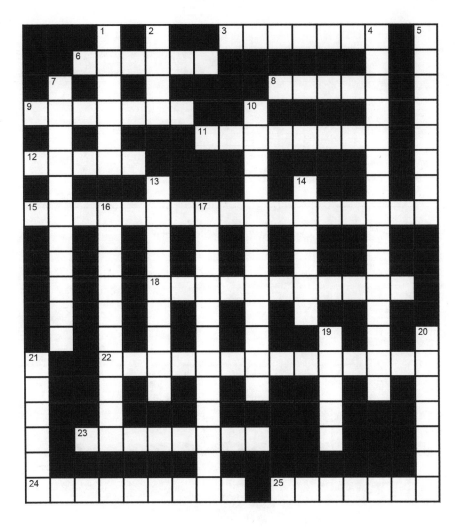

Across

3 Raiders division (3,4)
6 Bills owners, Kim and Terry (6)
8 2020 MVP GB, _____ Rodgers (5)
9 Browns DE, Myles (7)
11 Also known as "four-down territory" (4,4)
12 1985 MVP LAR, Marcus _____ (5)
15 Won 5 Superbowls (3,9,5)
18 Eagles coach 1976- 1982, later won SB with Rams (4,7)
22 2021 1st overall pick, QB, Jaguars (6,8)
23 SB VI MVP, DAL QB, Roger _____ (8)
24 Single season TD reception record (23) (5,4)
25 SB XXXVII MVP, TB, Dexter (7)

Down

1 Titans 4x Pro Bowl RB, Eddie (6)
2 Kick in which ball is dropped and kicked before it reaches ground (4)
4 Derrick Henry's team (9,6)
5 Raiders (3,5)
7 The player currently in possession of ball (4,7)
10 Jaguars (12)
13 Most receiving yards in Dolphins history (4,5)
14 SB XXXI MVP, Desmond (6)
16 A foul in which an offensive player moves before the ball is snapped (5,5)
17 Beat NE in Super Bowl XX (7,5)
19 Bengals owner, Mike (5)
20 Jets coach in 2010 (3,4)
21 John Elway played here (6)

Puzzle #8

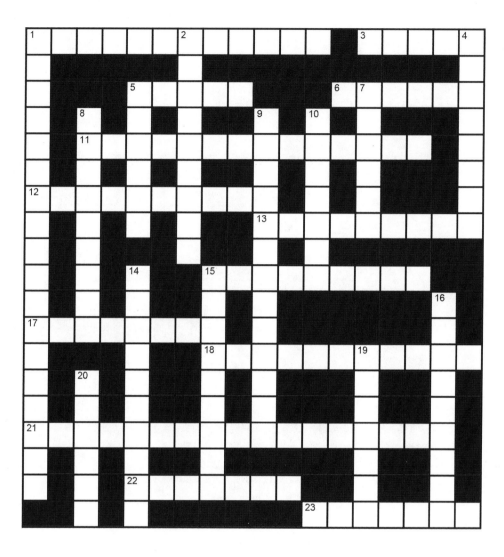

Across

1. Eagles coach since 2021 (4,8)
3. _____ kick; punt of kickoff intentionally kicked with less than full force (5)
5. Bullet Bob (5)
6. A player who holds the ball upright for a place kick (6)
11. 1986 DPOY NYG (8,6)
12. Texans coach in 2022 (5,5)
13. 3x Pro Bowl QB, KC, 49ers (4,5)
15. Kicker Patriots and Colts, Adam _____ (9)
17. Falcons RB 1994 - 2001, Jamal _____ (8)
18. Packers coach since 2019 (4,7)
21. OLB (7,10)
22. When a quarterback sees a blitz coming and quickly passes to a receiver running a short route (3,4)
23. _____ down; a down in which a pass is likely to be attempted (7)

Down

1. Beat STL in Super Bowl XXXVI (3,7,8)
2. 1979 DPOY TB DE Lee _____ (3,6)
4. Brother vs brother Super Bowl (8)
5. SB V MVP, DAL, Chuck (6)
7. Titans were previously known as the _____ (6)
8. Saban worked under Belichick in _____ (9)
9. Browns QB as of 2022 (7,6)
10. Broncos coach in 2022, Nathaniel (7)
14. Touchdown passes Dan Marino had in 1984 (5,5)
15. SB 50 MVP, DEN LB (3,6)
16. Legendary Browns head coach (4,5)
19. Blew 28-3 lead (7)
20. Julio Jones traded from Falcons to _____ (6)

Puzzle #9

Across
1 Raiders owner, Mark _____ (5)
3 TE (5,3)
7 Beat MIA in Super Bowl XVII (10,8)
10 1st Bronco with 15 + sacks in a season, 1992, Simon (8)
11 Broncos coach 1981 - 1992 (3,6)
12 Bucs HOF safety, now 49ers front office (4,5)
13 2000 MVP STL, Marshall _____ (5)
14 SB LVI MVP, LAR (6,4)
16 SB XLVI MVP, NYG (3,7)
18 MLB (6,10)
19 SB II MVP, Green Bay, Bart _____ (5)
21 Raiders QB in 2022 (5,4)
22 Mark Davis dad (2,5)
23 ARI and BAL WR, Anquan (6)

Down
1 Saints passing yards record, _____ Brees (4)
2 PIT "Mean" (3,6)
4 Won Super Bowl I (5,3,7)
5 Cover of Madden 2002, MIN (5,9)
6 Packers coach 1959 - 1967 (5,8)
8 2019 DPOY NE (7,7)
9 Beat Dallas in Super Bowl XIII (8)
12 SB XXXIII MVP, DEN (4,5)
15 SB XL MVP, PIT WR (5,4)
17 The field of play; a football field (8)
20 2016 MVP ATL, Matt _____ (4)

Puzzle #10

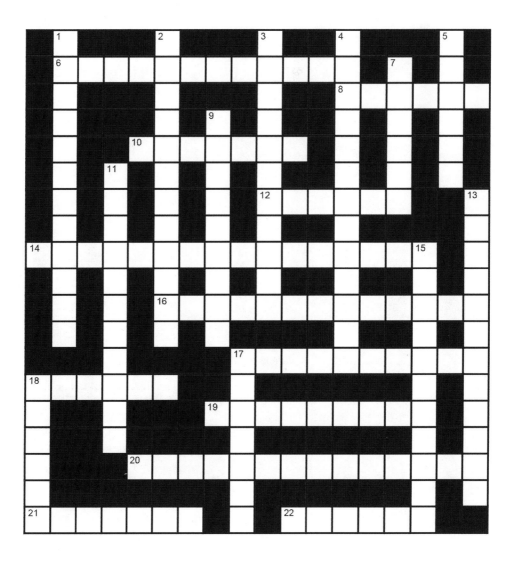

Across

6 Pass _____; when player illegally hinders eligible receiver's opportunity to catch pass (12)

8 SEA to DEN QB, Russell _____ (6)

10 Jets LB, hit that injured Drew Bledsoe (2,5)

12 Lou "The Toe" Groza position (6)

14 Beat IND in Super Bowl XLIV (3,7,6)

16 Colts career rushing leader (8,5)

17 Steelers (10)

18 Bengals and Patriots RB, Corey (6)

19 Booger (9)

20 KC RB nicknamed "The Nigerian Nightmare" (9,5)

21 Seahawks (7)

22 2018 DPOY LAR, Aaron _____ (6)

Down

1 Tuna (4,8)

2 2022 1st overall pick, DE, JAX (6,6)

3 Browns QB who led them to 3 AFC champ games in the 1980s (6,5)

4 Beat BUF in Super Bowl XXV (3,4,6)

5 Ravens were previously the _____ (6)

7 Buccaneers owner last name (6)

9 "The Galloping Ghost" (3,6)

11 2006 DPOY MIA (5,6)

13 ESPN reporter, breaks trades and signings (4,8)

15 Drafted 1st overall in 2010, Rams QB (3,8)

17 Interception returned to passing team's end zone for a touchdown (4,3)

18 Cowboys (6)

Puzzle #11

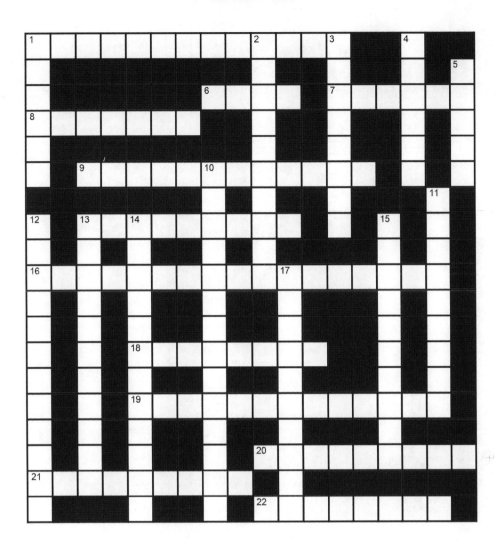

Across

1. Chargers QB, _____ _____ (6,7)
6. Drafted 1st overall in 2012, Colts QB, Andrew _____ (4)
7. Dolphins QB number 13, Dan _____ (6)
8. Chargers division (3,4)
9. 49ers coach since 2017 (4,8)
13. Madden 11 cover, Saints (4,5)
16. Scored 55 points in a Super Bowl (3,9,5)
18. 1991 DPOY NO LB Pat _____ (8)
19. 2005 DPOY CHI (5,8)
20. Dolphins HOF QB (3,6)
21. Peyton Manning college (9)
22. Kyler Murray college (8)

Down

1. Had 20.5 sacks in 2012 and 2014, HOU (2,4)
2. Tampa Bay (10)
3. SB XXXVIII MVP, NE (3,5)
4. Won Super Bowl as Bucs coach, previously coached the Cardinals (6)
5. 1994 MVP SF, Steve _____ (5)
10. Cowboys traded him to MIN for 5 players and 8 draft picks (8,6)
11. Former Commanders owner (3,6)
12. Cowboys head coach 2011-2019 (5,7)
13. Saints coach promoted from DC in 2022 (6,5)
14. Fumbled just before winning touchdown 1987 AFC champ game, CLE (7,5)
15. Cowboys kicker who was the 1st to kick 3 60+ yard FGs (5,5)
17. A defensive back who lines up near the line of scrimmage across from a wide receiver (10)

Puzzle #12

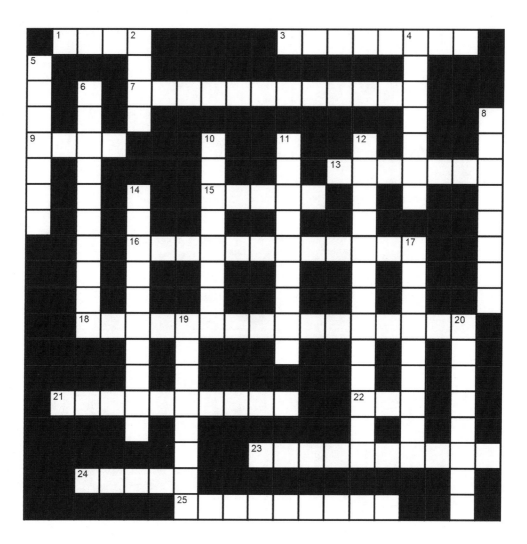

Across

1 Number of Super Bowls the Vikings appeared in, in 1970s (4)
3 Bears owner, Virginia Halas (8)
7 Hall of Fame wide receiver known as 'The Playmaker' (7,5)
9 HOF, Bills, Andre ____ (4)
13 Beat PHI in Super Bowl XV (7)
15 Field goal is worth this many points (5)
16 City that hosts the annual NFL Scouting Combine (12)
18 This team won Super Bowl LIV in 2020, ending a 50-year championship drought (6,4,6)
21 The NFL's policy to ensure minority candidates are considered for coaching and executive positions (6,4)
22 Number of losing seasons Dolphins had under Don Shula (3)
23 City that hosted the first Super Bowl (3,7)
24 Dolphins (5)
25 He holds the record for most career passing yards (4,5)

Down

2 The NFL team that returned to Los Angeles in 2016 after a 21-year absence (4)
4 1992 DPOY SEA DT Cortez (7)
5 WR traded from Titans to Eagles in 2022 (2,5)
6 First NFL player to kneel during the national anthem to protest racial injustice (10)
8 City that the Raiders franchise moved to in 2020 (3,5)
10 Team with the most Super Bowl appearances as of 2021 (8)
11 He famously guaranteed a victory before Super Bowl III and then delivered (3,6)
12 Cowboys FB nicknamed "Moose" (5,8)
14 SB XLII MVP, NYG (3,7)
17 Saints Stadium (9)
19 Chiefs coach since 2013 (4,4)
20 Beat MN in Super Bowl IX (8)

Puzzle #13

Across

- **4** Cowboys owner (5,5)
- **8** LT (4,6)
- **10** Falcons QB 75-85, ROY, 2x Pro Bowl, Steve (10)
- **12** 2017 DPOY LAR, _____ Donald (5)
- **13** Every touchdown is _____ (8)
- **14** HOU (7,6)
- **16** 2015 DPOY HOU (2,4)
- **17** Former Bills QB and Bob Dole's running mate in 1996 (4,4)
- **19** SB LIV MVP, KC, Patrick _____ (7)
- **20** Titans coach 1995-2010 (4,6)
- **22** Rams coach since 2017 (4,5)
- **23** "Hello friends…" CBS (3,5)
- **24** Packers division (3,5)
- **25** The Sheriff (7)

Down

- **1** Panthers first ever draft pick, QB, Kerry (7)
- **2** Former Patriots DC and Lions HC (4,8)
- **3** DT (9,6)
- **5** 1974 DPOY PIT DT (3,6)
- **6** SB XXI MVP, NYG QB, Phil _____ (5)
- **7** SB XII MVPs, DAL, Harvey _____, Randy _____ (7,5)
- **9** SB XI MVP, Raiders, Fred (11)
- **11** 1975 MVP MIN (4,9)
- **15** 1973 MVP BUF (2,7)
- **18** 1st QB to throw for over 5,000 yards in a season, Warren _____ (4)
- **21** Cover of Madden 07, SEA, _____ Alexander (5)

Puzzle #14

Across

1. SB XIII MVP, PIT QB (5,8)
4. SB XLIX MVP, NE (3,5)
5. A kick in which the ball is dropped and kicked once it hits the ground and before it hits it again (4,4)
11. 1969 MVP LAR (5,7)
12. Drafted Deion Sanders (7)
13. Beat MIN in Super Bowl IV (6,4,6)
15. _____ block; offensive player blocks defender moving back toward their own end zone (4-4)
17. Pro Bowl WR, Texans to Cardinals (7,7)
19. Famous singer that tried out for the Lions in 1970 (6,4)
20. SB XXXV MVP, BAL LB (3,5)
21. QB drafted 10th overall by the Jaguars in 2011 (7)

Down

2. 2021 MVP GB, Aaron _____ (7)
3. Jim Nantz broadcast partner before Romo (4,5)
5. 3x Pro Bowl QB, Vikings 1999-2005 (6,9)
6. 2016 DPOY OAK (6,4)
7. 1993 MVP DAL (6,5)
8. SB XXVII MVP, DAL QB (4,6)
9. Longtime Bengals coach with disappointing playoff record (6,5)
10. Packers to Raiders All Pro WR (7,5)
14. Cowboys DE, Demarcus (8)
16. Los Angeles (8)
18. Holds single game rushing record, _____ Peterson (6)

Puzzle #15

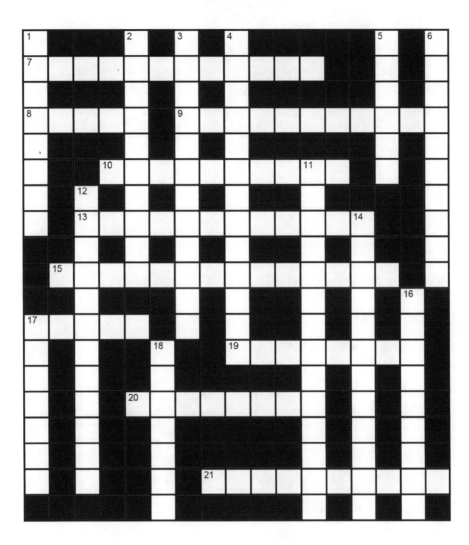

Across

7 Chargers RB (6,6)
8 Super Bowl trophy, _____ Lombardi trophy (5)
9 Darrelle Revis nickname (5,6)
10 Titans coach since 2018 (4,6)
13 Longtime Chargers QB drafted in 2004 (6,6)
15 Head coach, Chargers, Chiefs, Marty (14)
17 Falcons owner, Arthur (5)
19 Beat Rams in Super Bowl XIV (8)
20 Dolphins coach hired in 2022, Mike _____ (8)
21 The defensive linemen and linebackers (5,5)

Down

1 City Raiders moved to in 2020 (3,5)
2 Replaced Al Michaels on SNF (4,6)
3 49ers Pro Bowl TE (6,6)
4 Beat Green Bay in Super Bowl XXXII (6,7)
5 2014 DPOY HOU (2,4)
6 Bucs head coach promoted from DC in 2022 (4,6)
11 Cowboys, Patriots RB, OSU (7,7)
12 Offense, defense, and _____ (7,5)
14 Jerry Jones son (7,5)
16 Patriots/Broncos slot WR (3,6)
17 Cardinals owner, Michael (7)
18 Group of players on the field for a given play (7)

Puzzle #16

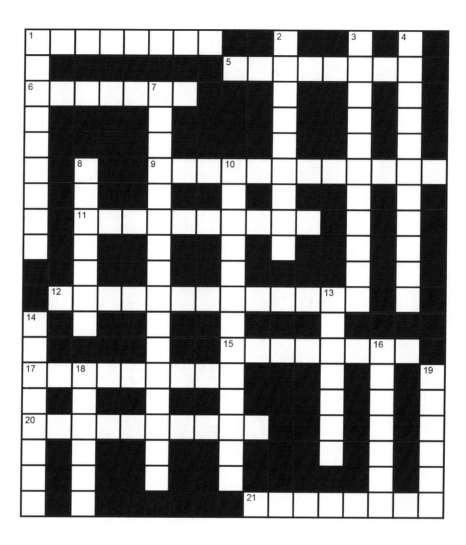

Across

1. 2012 MVP MIN, Adrian _____ (8)
5. Baker Mayfield college (8)
6. Type of block where player being blocked is pushed onto ground by blocker (7)
9. 1997 DPOY SF DT Dana (12)
11. Commanders DE, OSU (5,5)
12. Bills came back from down 32 to beat this team in the playoffs (7,6)
15. RB "Cadillac" (8)
17. Panthers coach since 2020 (4,5)
20. Longtime Cardinals receiver, Larry (10)
21. Matty Ice (4,4)

Down

1. Youth football league (3,6)
2. Rams original city (9)
3. Most career rushing yards in Commanders history (4,7)
4. Giants QB, Duke (6,5)
7. Beat SF in Super Bowl LIV (6,4,6)
8. Speedy WR best known as an Eagle, DeSean (7)
10. QB signed by HOU for 4 years and 72 million in 2016 (5,8)
13. Beat MIN in Super Bowl XI (7)
14. When quarterback fakes pass and keeps ball (4,4)
16. 1982 MVP WASH Kicker, Mark _____ (7)
18. Oilers changed name to (6)
19. 1977 MVP CHI, Walter _____ (6)

Puzzle #17

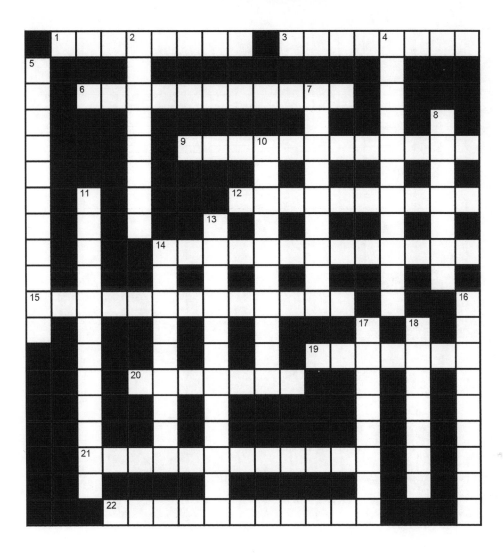

Across

1 Seattle (8)
3 1965 MVP CLE (3,5)
6 "The Catch" (6,5)
9 Chargers to Broncos RB (6,6)
12 Play where kicking team tries to recover kicked ball (6,4)
14 1988 MVP CIN (6,7)
15 Holds Chiefs record for most sacks, safeties, and forced fumbles, HOF 2009 (7,6)
19 Las Vegas (7)
20 Minnesota (7)
21 A penalty committed by either team before or after the play (4,4,4)
22 Jaguars to Rams, All Pro Cornerback (5,6)

Down

2 A play used as a last resort as time is running out in either of two halves (4,4)
4 Patriots owner (6,5)
5 Rams to Titans WR (6,5)
7 Riverboat Ron (3,6)
8 Joe Montana nickname (3,4)
10 Cover of Madden 08, TEN (5,5)
11 Length of NFL field (7,5)
13 1983 MVP WASH (3,9)
14 Area of an American football field behind the line of scrimmage (9)
16 Bills current QB (4,5)
17 Bills HOF QB (3,5)
18 Matthew Stafford college (7)

Puzzle #18

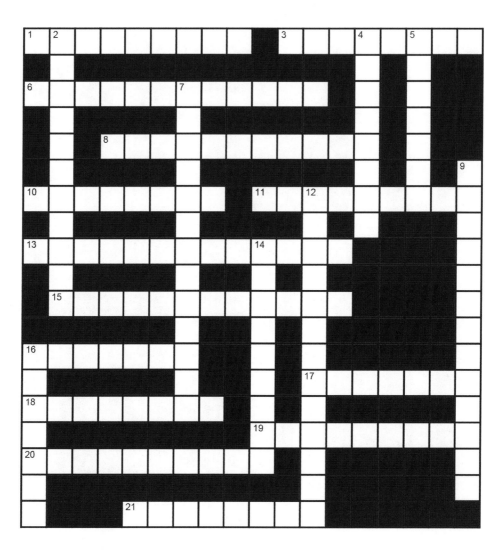

Across

1. A group of players that are responsible for recovering an onside kick (5,4)
3. Buccaneers (5,3)
6. "Legatron" (4,8)
8. First Cowboy to win MVP (6,5)
10. SB LI MVP, NE (3,5)
11. Stadium where power went out during the Super Bowl (9)
13. Beat MIA in Super Bowl VI (6,7)
15. Former Eagles and current Jaguars coach (4,8)
16. In 2005 Randy Moss was traded from the Vikings to the _____ (7)
17. Play called by the quarterback at the line of scrimmage to make a change from the play that was called in the huddle (7)
18. "Night Train (4,4)
19. Commanders coach since 2020 (3,6)
20. Drafted 1st overall in 2013, Chiefs tackle (4,6)
21. 4x Pro Bowl tackle, MIA, 1st overall pick 2008 (4,4)

Down

2. Rams All Pro DE (5,6)
4. Carolina (8)
5. Bills (7)
7. HOF Rams RB, averaged 5.6 yard per carry in 1984 (4,9)
9. A cornerback or safety position on the defensive team (9,4)
12. 2013 MVP DEN (6,7)
14. SB I MVP, Green Bay (4,5)
16. 2014 MVP GB, Aaron _____ (7)

Puzzle #19

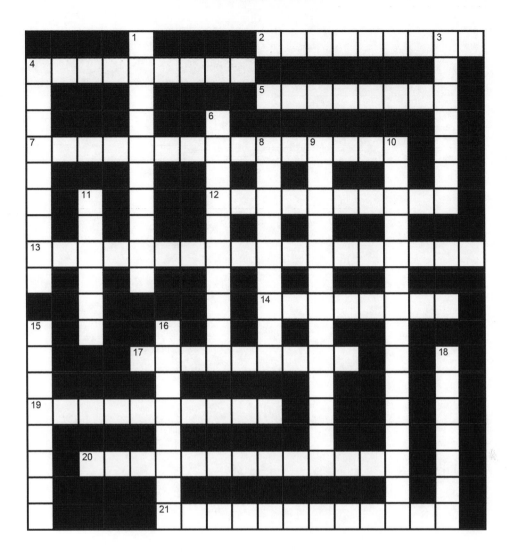

Across

2 Bears legendary HC (4,5)
4 "The Assassin", Raiders DB (4,5)
5 1963 MVP NYG (2,6)
7 Patriots stadium (8,7)
12 1985 DPOY CHI LN, Mike ___ (10)
13 Beat CAR in Super Bowl XXXVIII (3,7,8)
14 Saints division (3,5)
17 Number of teams in the NFL (6,3)
19 Browns QB, holds record for career average yards gained per pass attempt (4,6)
20 Drafted 1st overall in 2015, FSU QB (6,7)
21 Beat MIA in Super Bowl XIX (3,9)

Down

1 SB XXIX MVP, 49ers QB (5,5)
3 2013 DPOY CAR, Luke ___ (7)
4 1972 DPOY PIT DT (3,6)
6 1974 MVP OAK (3,7)
8 Coach of 2006 Super Bowl winning Colts (4,5)
9 Beat DEN in Super Bowl XII (6,7)
10 College team Jimmy Johnson coached (5,10)
11 2012 DPOY HOU (2,4)
15 Panthers (8)
16 Team that drafted Eli Manning (8)
18 New England traded Drew Bledsoe here (7)

Puzzle #20

Across

1. Saints QB for their first playoff win (5,6)
5. Jaguars owner (6,4)
10. SS (6,6)
12. 2006 MVP SD (9,9)
14. Packers Tackle, David _____ (9)
16. Al Davis son (4,5)
17. Bills division (3,4)
18. HOF Bills and Colts executive (4,6)
20. Cowboys QB , now CBS announcer (4,4)
21. Broncos Super Bowl winning coach, 1995 - 2008 (4,8)

Down

1. Offensive philosophy developed by San Diego Chargers head coach Don Coryell (3,7)
2. SB XVII MVP, WASH, John (7)
3. SB XVIII MVP, Raiders RB (6,5)
4. When player catches ball past line of scrimmage (9)
6. American Football Conference (3)
7. DET (7,5)
8. The corner of the field of play between the end zone and the 10 yard line (6,6)
9. Patriots coach since 2000 (9)
11. Dolphins QB, Alabama (3,10)
13. A ball which is no longer in play (4,4)
15. Ravens (9)
19. QB who retired at young age, Colts, Andrew _____ (4)

Puzzle #21

Across

1. Had amazing one handed catch as a rookie, NYG (5,7,2)
7. FB (8)
9. One of four periods of play (7)
10. Drew Brees original team (8)
11. Beat MIN in Super Bowl VIII (5,8)
13. Vikings owner (4,4)
14. Bills coach since 2017, Sean _____ (9)
17. Had 18 rushing touchdowns in 2008, CAR, DeAngelo (8)
18. Patriots division (3,4)
19. Jim Kelly nickname (7,3)
20. Raiders Pro Bowl TE, now on Giants (6,6)

Down

2. Trevor Lawrence college coach (4,7)
3. 1968 MVP BAL (4,7)
4. 2002 DROY, Panthers, later played for Bears (6,7)
5. Beat SEA in Super Bowl XL (8)
6. 2000 DPOY BAL (3,5)
8. 1989 1st overall pick, Dallas (4,6)
12. First openly gay player drafted in NFL (7,3)
13. Bengals coach since 2019 (3,6)
15. Chiefs owner (5,4)
16. Legendary Cowboys coach (3,6)

Puzzle #22

Across

1. HOF Bills RB (2,7)
6. Broncos stadium (4,4)
7. The final of a set of four downs (6,4)
10. Al Davis catchphrase (4,3,4)
13. Cover of Madden 2003, STL Rams (8,5)
15. QB drafted in 1st round in 2012 by CLE, unusually old (7,6)
18. Jets coach since 2021 (6,5)
19. PIT (10,8)
20. 1980 MVP CLE (5,4)
21. Formation with three running backs aligned behind quarterback in straight line (8)

Down

2. QB who led the Texans to their 1st ever winning record (4,6)
3. Patriots (3,7)
4. Packers fans (11)
5. Seahawks coach for 1st playoff win, 1983 (5,4)
8. CAR (8,8)
9. Patriots to 49ers QB (5,9)
11. "The refrigerator" (7,5)
12. 1996 DPOY BUF (5,5)
14. Atlanta Falcons stadium sponsor, car (8)
16. Seahawks division (3,4)
17. Super Bowl LV MVP, TB (3,5)

Puzzle #23

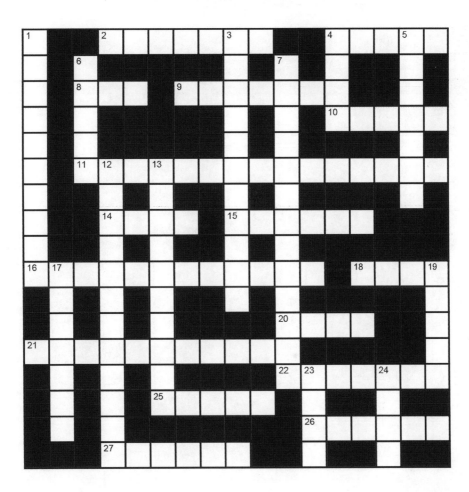

Across

2 Bengal that dropped a game winning INT in Super Bowl, Lewis (7)
4 Detroit (5)
8 Tom Landry always wore this on the sideline (3)
9 Seahawks WR, DK (7)
10 Number of time outs a team gets per half (5)
11 Nickname for Cowboys defense in the 1960s and 1970s (8,7)
14 Ezekiel Elliot nickname (4)
15 Steelers ownership family (6)
16 Scored 27 touchdowns in 2003, at the time a record, Chiefs (6,6)
18 Only team to win championships while representing 3 different cities (4)
20 In 2008 the Lions won ___ games (4)
21 1993 1st overall pick, Patriots (4,7)
22 Rams division (3,4)
25 Falcons LB 66-76, Tommy (5)
26 HOF Colts QB, Johnny (6)
27 1984 DPOY SEA S Kenny (6)

Down

1 1999 DPOY TB (6,4)
3 Seahawks coach since 2010 (4,7)
4 Steve Young is _____ handed (4)
5 Cowboys division (3,4)
6 Round Joe Montana was drafted (5)
7 UK QB, Hefty Lefty, NYG backup (5,8)
12 Hall of Fame Browns TE, now Ravens front office (5,7)
13 Steelers coach since 2007 (4,6)
17 Jets and Bills head coach (3,4)
19 SB VII MVP, MIA, Jake (5)
23 Number of QBs drafted ahead of Marino (4)
24 Eagles and Cardinals TE, Zach (4)

Puzzle #24

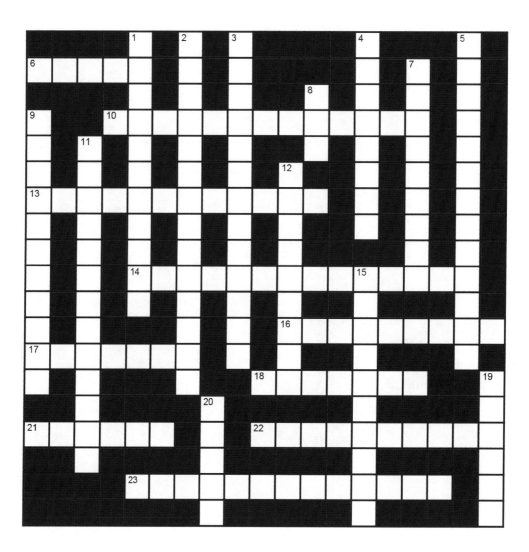

Across

6 Packers QB number 4, _____ Favre (5)

10 Matt Ryan college (6,7)

13 Rushed for 2,006 yards in 2009, TEN (5,7)

14 2001 DPOY NYG (7,7)

16 Arizona (9)

17 Rushed for 1,000 yards in his 1st 9 career games, DAL, Ezekiel _____ (7)

18 Dallas (7)

21 NFL career rushing yards record, _____ Smith (6)

22 Former red headed Bengals quarterback (4,6)

23 1991 MVP BUF (7,6)

Down

1 Beat TEN in Super Bowl XXXIV (2,5,4)

2 Team that originally drafted John Elway (9,5)

3 Chargers coach fired in 2023 (7,6)

4 Beat ARI in Super Bowl XLIII (8)

5 Viking coach hired in 2022 (5,9)

7 SB III MVP, NYJ (3,6)

8 Won 2 SB MVPS, NYG, _____ Manning (3)

9 Super Bowl clinching pick six, Saints vs Colts (5,6)

11 Drafted 1st overall in 2006, HOU (5,8)

12 QB who had historic postseason run in 2012 (3,6)

15 1993 DPOY PIT CB (3,7)

19 2nd overall pick 1999 draft, PHI QB, Donovan _____ (6)

20 Cover of Madden 09, NYJ (5)

Puzzle #25

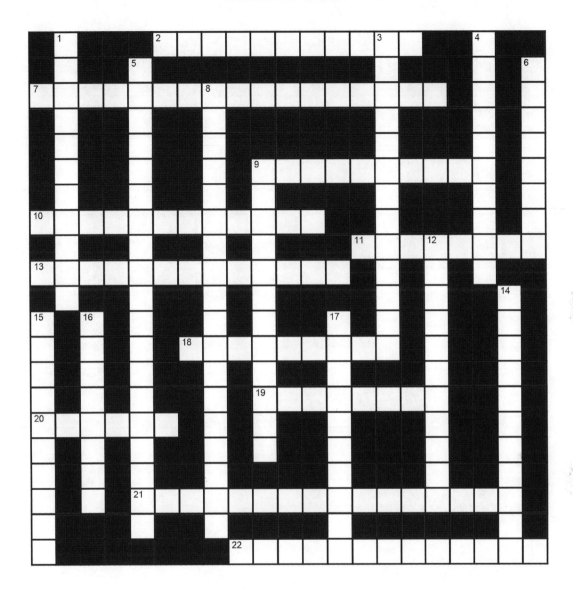

Across
- **2** SB XXXIX MVP NE WR (5,6)
- **7** IND (12,5)
- **9** SB XVI MVP, 49ers (3,7)
- **10** 2011 MVP GB (5,7)
- **11** Historic play in 1981 NFC championship game (3,5)
- **13** Won Super Bowl VII (5,8)
- **18** The first of a set of four downs (5,4)
- **19** Titans division (3,5)
- **20** Cover of Madden 2001, TEN, Eddie _____ (6)
- **21** Washington rookie phenom QB in 2012 (6,7,3)
- **22** Heisman trophy winner drafted by CLE in 2014 (6,7)

Down
- **1** Retired at halftime of a game, Bills (6,5)
- **3** "Megatron" (6,7)
- **4** FS (4,6)
- **5** JAX (12,7)
- **6** Bengals division (3,5)
- **8** Beat NE in Super Bowl LII (12,6)
- **9** Most career yards passing in Commanders history (3,9)
- **12** Ochocinco (4,7)
- **14** 1998 DPOY GB (6,5)
- **15** 1st Brown inducted into Hall of Fame (4,6)
- **16** Falcons division (3,5)
- **17** Physical control of ball after pass or fumble (10)

Puzzle #26

Across

1. "Broadway" (3,6)
6. Holds record for most receptions (5,4)
8. Beat BUF in Super Bowl XXVII (6,7)
12. Holds Colts record for passing yards in a season (6,4)
14. Threw a league high 75 INTs between 2014 and 2018, Jaguars (5,7)
15. 49ers division (3,4)
17. Drafted 1st overall in 2014, HOU DE (8,7)
20. Eagles owner (7,5)
21. Joe Namath was drafted by this team (9)
22. Giants WR, salsa dance (6,4)

Down

1. Jacksonville (7)
2. 1st Jaguars QB to pass for more than 4,000 yards in a season (4,7)
3. SB XIV MVP, PIT QB (5,8)
4. Drafted number 1 overall by NE in 1971, later won SB MVP on the Raiders (3,8)
5. 1958 MVP (3,5)
7. Only player with 12,000 rushing yards and 6,000 receiving yards (8,5)
9. Barry Sanders had record _____ straight 100+ yard games (8)
10. Packers QB number 12 (5,7)
11. Retired pro bowl LB, Boston college, Panthers (4,7)
13. Chargers and Patriots safety, won 2 Super Bowls (6,8)
16. Air Coryell (8)
18. _____ team; team with possession of ball (9)
19. Dolphins Division (3,4)

Puzzle #27

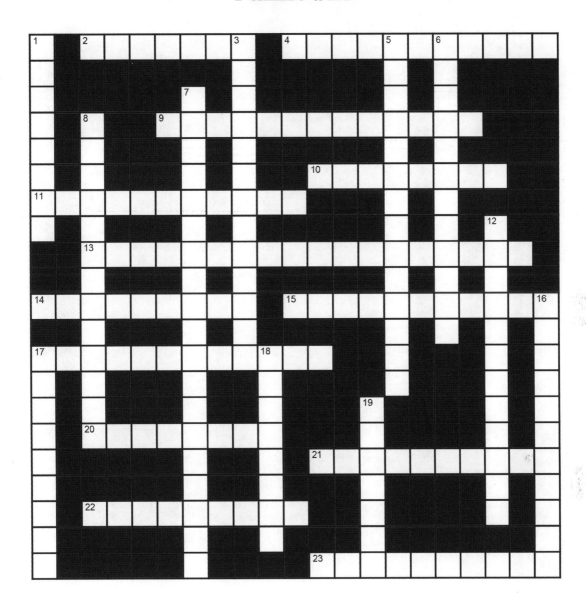

Across

2 Missed GW FG, Bills Super Bowl, Scott _____ (7)
4 Giants coach hired in 2022 (5,6)
9 2008 DPOY PIT (5,8)
10 Steelers division (3,5)
11 Eagles RB as of 2023 (6,5)
13 LAC (3,7,8)
14 49ers WR, some consider him the best WR ever (5,4)
15 QB (11)
17 2010 DPOY PIT (4,8)
20 SEA (8)
21 Chad Johnson number (6,4)
22 First 4,000 yard passer in NFL history, NYJ (3,6)
23 Commanders (10)

Down

1 TB12 (3,5)
3 The team that begins a play from scrimmage not in possession of the ball (9,4)
5 Before a game this song is sung (8,6)
6 Holds record for most passes without an INT (5,7)
7 Lost 2017 AFC Championship game to NE (12,7)
8 Pro Bowl DE, Patriots to Cardinals (8,5)
12 Ravens head coach when they won their first Super Bowl (5,7)
16 1981 MVP CIN (3,8)
17 Vikings QB number 10 (9)
18 Colts division (3,5)
19 Became a team in 1995, AFC South (7)

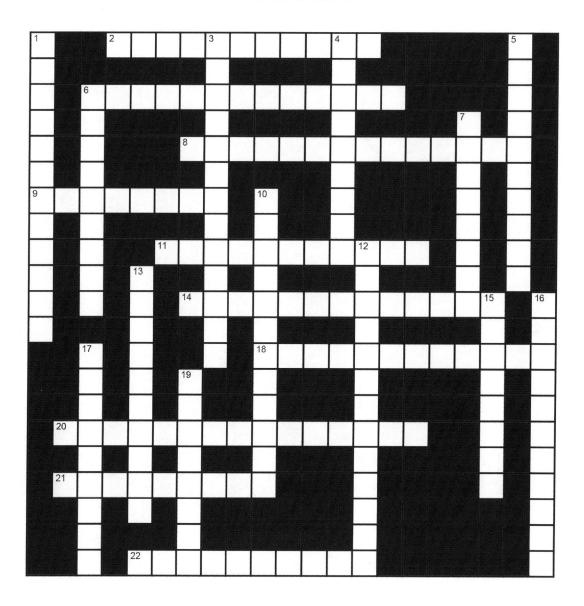

Puzzle #28

Across

2 "Crazylegs" LAR WR (5,6)
6 Patriots WR number 11, SB MVP (6,7)
8 WR traded from Texans to Cardinals (7,7)
9 Cover of Madden 2005, BAL (3,5)
11 The first working day following the final Sunday of the National Football League season (5,6)
14 Undefeated in 1972 (5,8)
18 CHI (7,5)
20 Drafted 1st overall in 2009, DET (7,8)
21 1987 MVP DEN (4,5)
22 Chargers (3,7)

Down

1 Giants coach in 80s and 90s (4,8)
3 Falcons won their 1st ever game at this famous baseball stadium (6,7)
4 Panthers QB in Super Bowl 50 (3,6)
5 Scored winning touchdown to complete 28-3 comeback in Super Bowl 51 (5,5)
6 Most receptions NFL history (5,4)
7 1957 MVP (3,5)
10 Former Packers and current Cowboys coach (4,8)
12 Beat BUF in Super Bowl XXVIII (6,7)
13 SB XIX MVP, 49ers (3,7)
15 Legion of Boom (8)
16 Longtime Cowboys TE in the Romo era (5,6)
17 A play where the quarterback hands the ball off to a wide receiver (3,6)
19 Pittsburgh (8)

Puzzle #29

Across

- **2** 1st black coach to win a Super Bowl (4,5)
- **4** 21 rushing TDs and 2,008 rushing yards in 1998, DEN (7,5)
- **7** Timer used to increase pace of game (4,5)
- **9** Chargers Pro Bowl WR (6,5)
- **11** Eagles trick play in Super Bowl (6,7)
- **13** PHI (12,6)
- **17** 1966 MVP GB (4,5)
- **18** Vikings division (3,5)
- **19** OBJ (5,7,2)
- **20** Set the record for most total touchdowns (31) scored in a season in 2006 (9,9)
- **21** Head Coach from 1973-1994, Rams, Bills, Seahawks (5,4)
- **22** 2007 DPOY IND (3,7)

Down

- **1** "The Playmaker" (7,5)
- **3** Saints (3,7)
- **5** Threw interception on 1 yard line, Super Bowl (7,6)
- **6** Lions coach since 2021 (3,8)
- **8** Eagles QB who got injured during 2017 Super Bowl year (6,5)
- **10** Amari Cooper team as of 2022 (9,6)
- **12** RT (5,6)
- **14** Lions "Flying Dutchman" (5,5)
- **15** Bought Cowboys in 1989 (5,5)
- **16** Unexpected punt (5,4)

Puzzle #30

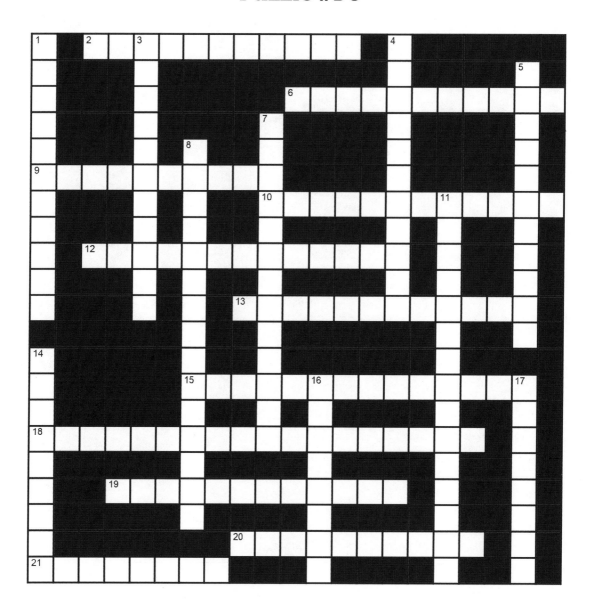

Across

2 PHI to IND to WASH QB (6,5)
6 Cardinals quarterback as of 2022 (5,6)
9 Jaguars coach fired after coaching one season in 2021 (5,5)
10 Steelers and Bucs WR, AB (7,5)
12 Titans QB, previously MIA (4,9)
13 Beat CIN in Super Bowl XXIII (3,9)
15 Rushed for 296 yards in a game as a rookie in 2007 (6,8)
18 Beat OAK in Super Bowl XXXVII (5,3,10)
19 LAR LB, "Hacksaw" (4,8)
20 Richard Sherman drafted in this round (5,5)
21 Ravens HOF LB, Won Super Bowl his last season (3,5)

Down

1 Jaguars Head Coach 1995-2002, Won 2 Super Bowls with Giants (3,8)
3 RB (7,4)
4 Broke Walter Payton's single game rushing record in 2000, CIN (5,6)
5 Bills owner 1960-2014 (5,6)
7 "Honey Badger" (6,7)
8 Joined NFL in 1976, not the Bucs (7,8)
11 BAL (9,6)
14 1962 MVP GB (3,6)
16 Panthers division (3,5)
17 Bears division (3,5)

Puzzle #31

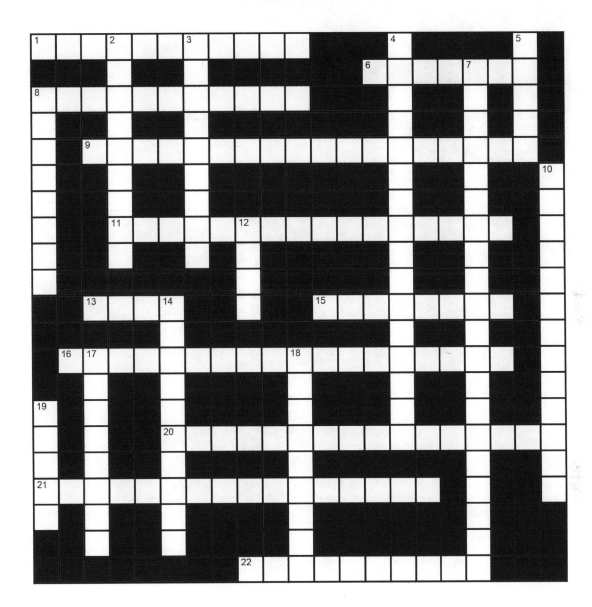

Across

1 Legally changed his name to match jersey number (4,7)
6 Titans drafted him high in the draft, Oregon QB (7)
8 Holds Vikings record for most passing yards in a single game (1986) (5,6)
9 Beat KC in Super Bowl LV (5,3,10)
11 RGIII (6,7,3)
13 Fired as Cowboys coach during the 2010 season, _____ Phillips (4)
15 1st overall pick 1999, Bust, CLE (3,5)
16 Chargers HOF RB (9,9)
20 NO (3,7,6)
21 Brady beat this team to win his second ring (8,8)
22 LB (10)

Down

2 Only person to coach 2 expansion teams in their inaugural season, CAR, HOU (3,6)
3 Patriots player later charged with murder, Aaron _____ (9)
4 KC (6,4,6)
5 Chargers franchise leader in receptions, receiving yards, and receiving TDs (5)
7 OC (9,11)
8 2017 MVP NE (3,5)
10 Gronk (3,10)
12 Rams team nicknamed when Kurt Warner was the QB, Greatest Show on _____ (4)
14 1st overall pick in 2004 draft, Chargers, Ole Miss (3,7)
17 Browns division (3,5)
18 Holds Chargers single season rushing record (9)
19 Seahawks RB, Beast Mode (5)

Puzzle #32

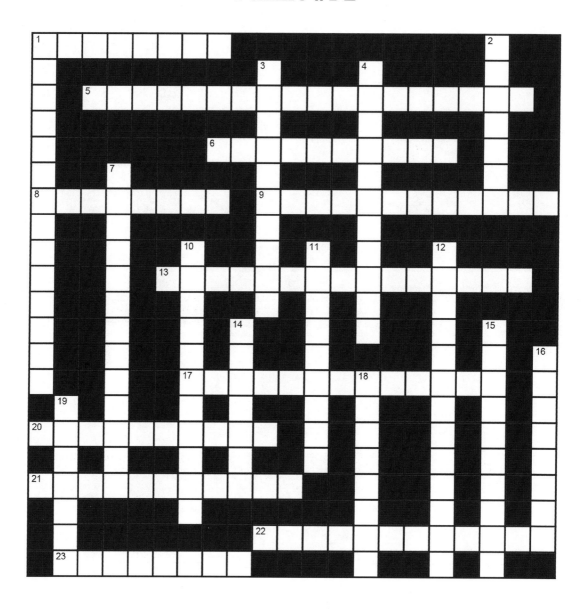

Across

1. Ravens division (3,5)
5. Beat Denver in Super Bowl XXII (10,8)
6. WR stopped on 1 yard line to end the Super Bowl, TEN/STL (5,5)
8. Bengals QB in Super Bowl XVI, Ken ___ (8)
9. Beat DEN in Super Bowl XXIV (3,9)
13. Won their first Super Bowl 43-8 (7,8)
17. Beat NE in Super Bowl XLII (3,4,6)
20. Jets QB as of 2022 (4,6)
21. 1993 1st overall pick, Patriots (4,7)
22. Nicknamed 'T.O.' (7,5)
23. 1st overall pick 1999, bust, CLE (3,5)

Down

1. ATL (7,7)
2. 1994 DPOY SF, Deion ___ (7)
3. Longtime Pro Bowl Panthers WR (5,5)
4. NYJ (3,4,4)
7. 1978 MVP PIT (5,8)
10. Rams player selected to 14 consecutive Pro Bowls, 1962-1975 (6,5)
11. Thomas 'Hollywood' ___ (9)
12. Broke Jerry Rice's season receiving yards record in 2012 (6,7)
14. In 1995 Deion Sanders left the 49ers for the ___ (7)
15. City Raiders moved to in 1982 (3,7)
16. Caught Kurt Warners 1st career interception, HOF BAL (3,5)
18. Chiefs and Falcons HOF TE, Tony ___ (8)
19. Drafted 1st overall in 2017, CLE DE (7)

Puzzle #33

Across

1 Jerry Jones lured this coach out of retirement in 2003 (4,8)
3 Eagles coach, won Super Bowl LII (8)
6 Browns player voted to Pro Bowl every year he played (3,5)
10 "The Bus" (6,6)
13 First QB to throw for 400+ yards in his 1st game, CAR (3,6)
14 Saints franchise leader in receiving yards and touchdowns (7,7)
16 First team Belichick was the head coach of (9,6)
17 1987 DPOY PHI (6,5)
18 2010 MVP NE (3,5)
19 Trevor Lawrence college coach (4,7)
20 Resigned as Raiders coach after controversial leaked emails (3,6)
21 WAS (10,10)

Down

1 Hoodie (4,9)
2 Ravens QB in 2000 SB winning season (5,6)
4 Cover of Madden 06, PHI (7,6)
5 Beat NE in Super Bowl XLVI (3,4,6)
7 Cowboys QB on 1st SB winning team (5,8)
8 Doug Flutie college (6,7)
9 Cowboys record for most consecutive games with a catch (5,6)
11 The 1999 Jaguars went 15-3 and lost all 3 games to this team (9,6)
12 Eagles traded for this HOF WR prior to 2004 season (7,5)
14 2009 MVP IND, Peyton _____ (7)
15 49ers QB 1961-1973, MVP, #12 (4,6)

Puzzle #34

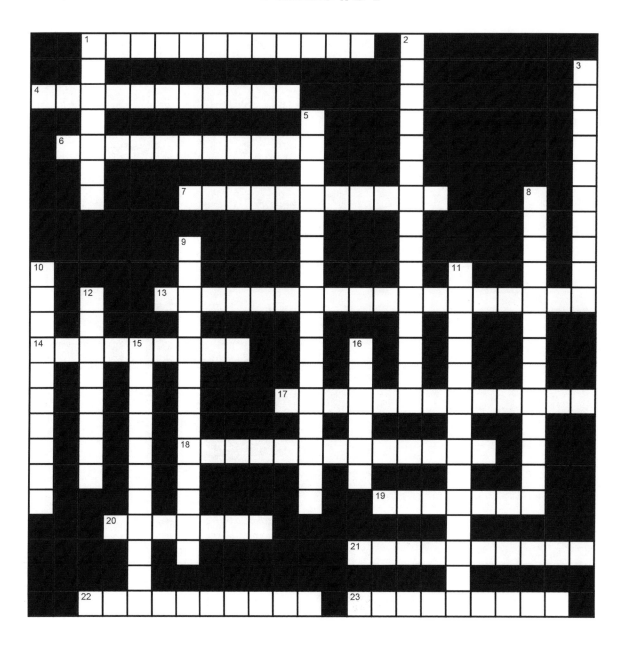

Across
1 Eagles (12)
4 Cover of Madden 2004, ATL (7,4)
6 PSI levels (11)
7 The area between both the goal lines and the sidelines (5,2,4)
13 Gronk came out of retirement to join this team (5,3,10)
14 Giants DC in 80s and 90s (9)
17 America's Team (6,7)
18 2008 MVP IND (6,7)
19 Beat PIT in Super Bowl XXX (7)
20 1998 1st overall pick (7)
21 1989 MVP SF (3,7)
22 Player that guards a wide receiver (10)
23 Drafted 1st overall in 2016, Rams QB (5,4)

Down
1 Beat NE in Super Bowl XXXI (7)
2 Beat PIT in Super Bowl XLV (5,3,7)
3 Brady joined this team after New England (10)
5 Archie Manning team (3,7,6)
8 DEN (6,7)
9 Chiefs traded Tyreek Hill to this team (5,8)
10 Patriots stadium location (10)
11 Played in 201 consecutive games, Rams (4,10)
12 Only team to complete a perfect season (8)
15 DC, defensive _____ (11)
16 Bills lost to them twice in the Super Bowl, ____ Cowboys (6)

Puzzle #35

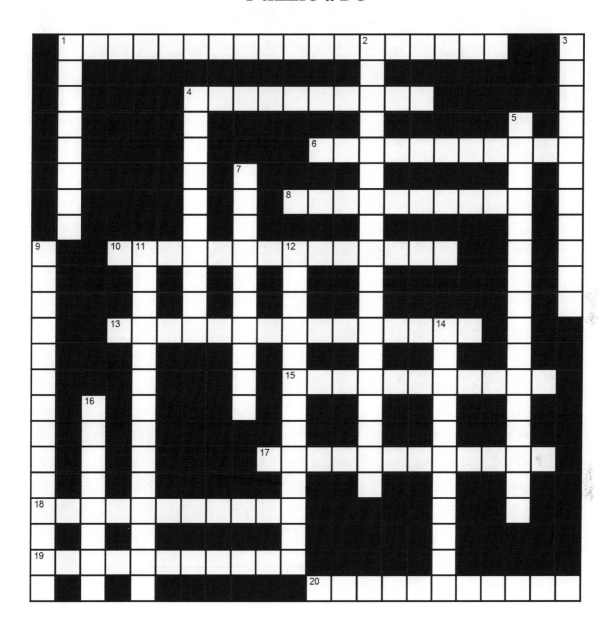

Across
1. Beat PHI in Super Bowl XXXIX (3,7,8)
4. Joe Buck broadcast partner (4,6)
6. Player that throws the football (11)
8. Rams (3,7)
10. Cardinals coach 2019-2022 (5,9)
13. Super Bowl II winner (5,3,7)
15. Player that usually runs with the football (7,4)
17. WR (4,8)
18. Bengals Pro Bowl RB, Won Super Bowl with NE (5,6)
19. Lost the AFC Championship game in 2009 and 2010 (3,4,4)
20. Cowboys QB as of 2022 (3,8)

Down
1. Lions division (3,5)
2. TB (5,3,10)
3. Only player from losing team to be named SB MVP, Dallas (5,6)
4. If a kickoff results in a touchback the offense will start on their own ____ (6,4)
5. The Packers defeated this team in the first ever Super Bowl (6,4,6)
7. Extra or fifth defensive back (6,4)
9. Originally drafted Brett Favre (7,7)
11. 1982 DPOY NYG (8,6)
12. NYG (3,4,6)
14. Had 21 sacks in 1987, PHI (6,5)
16. Number thirty-two Browns (3,5)

Puzzle #36

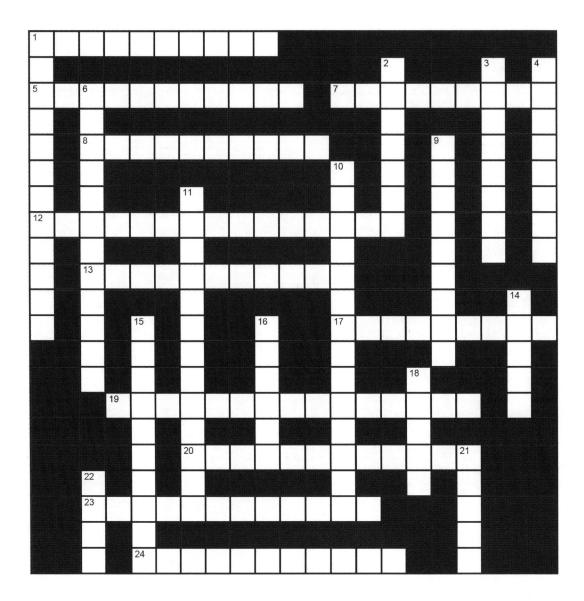

Across

1. 1992 MVP SF (5,5)
5. Giants share stadium with (3,4,4)
7. Rams to Lions QB (5,4)
8. A play in which the ball is passed directly to a player other than the quarterback by the center (6,4)
12. In the 1980s Denver beat this team 3 times in the AFC championship game (9,6)
13. Scored both Titans TDs in Super Bowl XXXIV (5,6)
17. Drafted 1st overall in 2011, CAR (3,6)
19. Bearded quarterback who went to Harvard (4,11)
20. T-Sizzle, Ravens (7,5)
23. "Primetime" (5,7)
24. Drafted 1st overall in 2019, ARI (5,6)

Down

1. Beat SD in Super Bowl XXIX (3,9)
2. Home games are played at high altitude (7)
3. 2007 MVP NE (3,5)
4. Jaguars division (3,5)
6. Player that usually catches the football (4,8)
9. Former Broncos and Bears QB (3,6)
10. L.T. Giants (8,6)
11. Gave infamous crab leg speech, Bucs (6,7)
14. Texans division, AFC ____ (5)
15. Coach of Broncos 2015 Super Bowl winning team (4,6)
16. 1st player to have 100+ rushing yards in his first 3 playoff games, HOU (6)
18. WR Vikings to Bills, Stefon ____ (5)
21. 1990 DPOY BUF, Bruce ____ (5)
22. Kicked 2 game winning field goals in the Super Bowl for the Patriots, ____ Vinatieri (4)

Puzzle #37

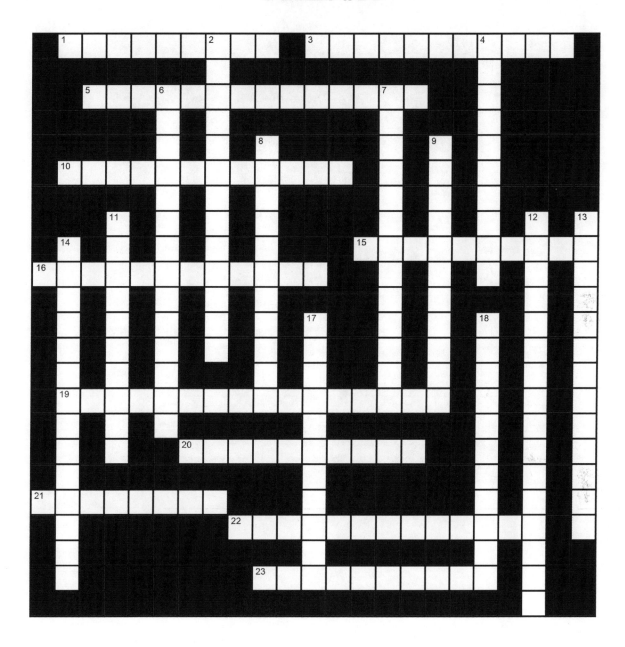

Across
1. Coach traded from Raiders to Bucs (3,6)
3. Originally named the New York Titans (3,4,4)
5. 1981 DPOY NYG (8,6)
10. Ravens coach since 2008 (4,8)
15. Bengals (10)
16. 1997 CO-MVP DET (5,7)
19. Traded for Marcus Allen and Joe Montana in 1993 (6,4,6)
20. Mark Sanchez Thanksgiving mishap (4,6)
21. Drafted pick 199 (3,5)
22. Coach throws flag (9,4)
23. Chiefs (6,4)

Down
2. Beat CAR in Super Bowl 50 (6,7)
4. SB XXIV MVP, 49ers (3,7)
6. CB from SEA Legion of Boom defense (7,7)
7. Players that protect the quarterback (9,4)
8. Most passes to start a career without an INT (3,8)
9. Vikings QB, previously Washington (4,7)
11. 1999 MVP STL (4,6)
12. Team that drafted Eli Manning (3,5,8)
13. Nick Saban coached this NFL team (5,8)
14. 2018 MVP KC (7,7)
17. 1st ever Jaguars head coach (3,8)
18. A play in which a pass is attempted (7,4)

Puzzle #38

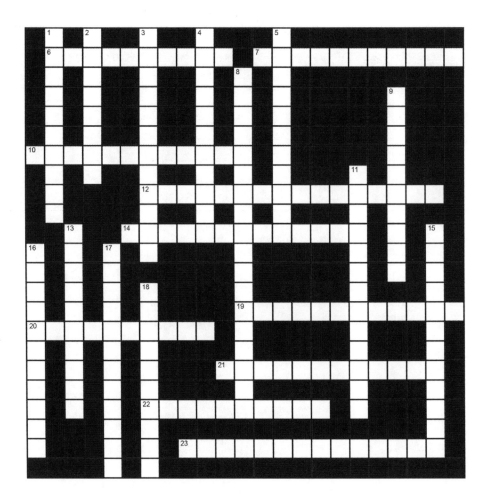

Across

6 1989 1st overall pick, Dallas (4,6)
7 Michael Vick went to jail for (3,8)
10 Jets owner (5,7)
12 NFC South Team founded in 1966 (3,7,6)
14 Joined NFL in 2002, AFC South (7,6)
19 Holds record for most career receiving yards by a TE (4,8)
20 Cardinals quarterback in SBXLIII vs PIT (4,6)
21 1967 MVP BAL (6,6)
22 Most career sacks (200) (5,5)
23 Chiefs All Pro QB (7,7)

Down

1 HOF QB Bucs traded in 1987 (5,5)
2 Oldest player as of 2022 (3,5)
3 Cowboys Super Bowl winning coach in the 1990s (5,7)
4 Highest passer rating for a rookie in history (3,8)
5 Caused a 34 minute delay in the BAL/SF Super Bowl (5,6)
8 Beat SEA in Super Bowl XLIX (3,7,8)
9 1990 MVP SF (3,7)
11 Beast Mode (8,5)
13 Rams WR and SB MVP (6,4)
15 2011 DPOY BAL (7,5)
16 Lions player who died on field during game, 1971 (5,6)
17 SB XXII MVP, WASH (4,8)
18 CB (10)

Puzzle #39

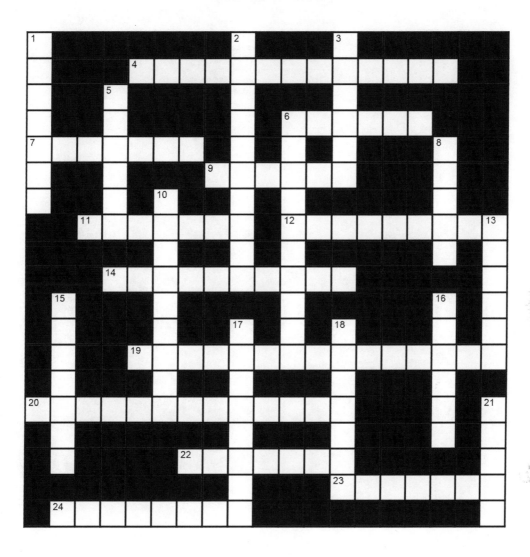

Across

4 The only NFL team to complete a perfect season, including the Super Bowl win. (5,8)

6 Saints owner, Gayle _____ (6)

7 Eagles division (3,4)

9 Baltimore (6)

11 Vikings WR, Adam _____ (7)

12 Titans (9)

14 Legendary quarterback known as 'The Comeback Kid.' (3,7)

19 This team's fans are known as the '12th Man' (7,8)

20 This quarterback is known for yelling 'Omaha' before the snap (6,7)

22 Annual event where NFL players demonstrate their skills in various competitions (3,4)

23 Kenny "The Snake" (7)

24 Eagles coach for Super Bowl XXXIX (4,4)

Down

1 Falcons (7)

2 2002 MVP OAK (4,6)

3 Chargers owner, Dean _____ (6)

5 Bengals all time leading scorer, kicker Jim _____ (6)

6 1997 CO-MVP GB (5,5)

8 Kordell Stewart's nickname (5)

10 Number of games in NFL regular season (9)

13 Philadelphia (6)

15 Beat Washington in Super Bowl XVIII (7)

16 2021 DPOY PIT (2,4)

17 Andrew Luck's college (8)

18 Cincinnati (7)

21 Chicago (5)

Puzzle #40

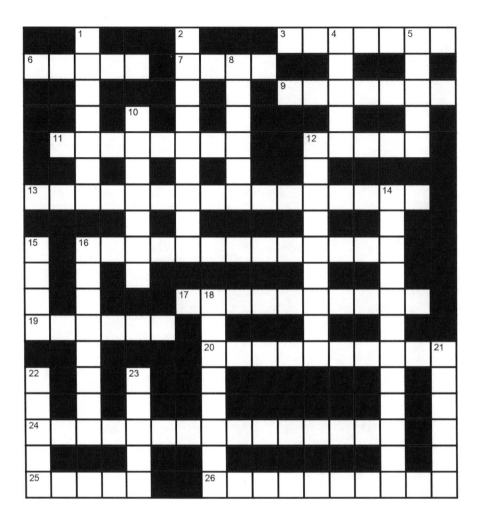

Across

3 Jets (3,4)
6 Earl Lambeau nickname (5)
7 Joe Buck left FOX for this network (4)
9 Bears (7)
11 Commanders WR, Terry (8)
12 Ravens single season rushing record, Jamal (5)
13 Bill Walsh offensive scheme (4,5,7)
16 HOF OL, 1st ever Ravens draft pick (8,5)
17 RB nicknamed "the Kansas Comet" (4,6)
19 Michael Vick team after Falcons (6)
20 "Deacon" (5,5)
24 LV (3,5,7)
25 Championships Otto Graham won (5)
26 Rich Eisen works for this network (3,7)

Down

1 Denver (7)
2 Controversial "catch" ruled incomplete in 2014 playoffs, DAL/GB (3,6)
4 Falcons Pro Bowl WR, Roddy (5)
5 3x Pro Bowl, ATL RB 82-88, Gerald (5)
8 Charles Tillman nickname (6)
10 Atlanta (7)
12 LG (4,5)
14 Beat CIN in Super Bowl XVI (3,9)
15 Times Peyton won MVP (4)
16 HOF Washington head coach (3,5)
18 SB XXV MVP, NYG, Ottis (8)
21 Titans owner. Amy Adams (6)
22 Buffalo (5)
23 Former Bengals Pro Bowl WR, A.J. (5)

Puzzle #41

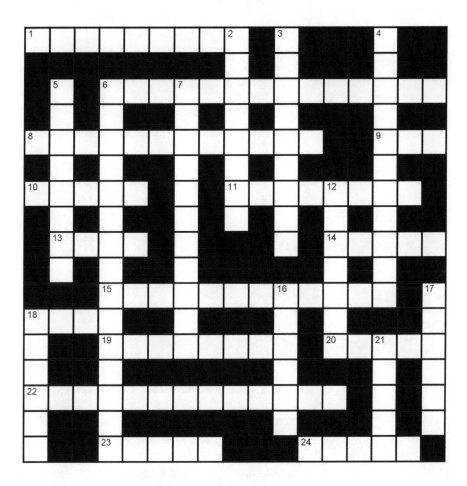

Across

1 Chiefs stadium (9)
6 Beat DAL in Super Bowl V (9,5)
8 Packers coach 1919-1949 (5,7)
9 A sharp change of direction by a running player (3)
10 Broncos owner, Joe (5)
11 A penalty called for an illegal block in which the blocked player is hit from behind at or below the waist (8)
13 Mike Ditka nickname (4)
14 A statistic referring to the number of times a rushing player attempts to advance the ball (5)
15 1979 MVP HOU Oilers (4,8)
18 Super Bowls 49ers won in the 1980s (4)
19 1973 DPOY MIA S Dick _____ (8)
20 Longtime Raven, Terrell (5)
22 Drafted 1st overall in 2018, CLE (5,8)
23 Round Tom Brady was drafted (5)
24 Broncos WR Jerry (5)

Down

2 The second extra, or sixth total, defensive back (4,4)
3 An arrangement of the offensive skill players (9)
4 A strategy that is based on low-risk plays in an effort to avoid losing possession of the ball (4,7)
5 Panthers single season passing yard record (8)
6 Beat NYG in Super Bowl XXXV (9,6)
7 Chiefs All Pro TE (6,5)
12 Green Bay (7)
16 P (6)
17 Pro Bowl Texans RB, Arian (6)
18 A ball that a player accidentally lost possession of (6)
21 Two of the five offensive line positions (5)

Puzzle #42

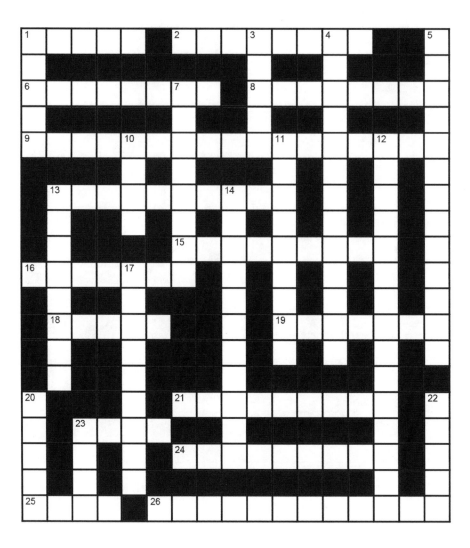

Across

1. An attempt to prevent a receiver from catching a pass (5)
2. Lions owner Sheila (4,4)
6. Had ball stripped away from him in Super Bowl while celebrating (4,4)
8. Alternate term for end zone (4,4)
9. Patriots kicker following Vinatieri departure (7,10)
13. 1970 MVP SF (4,6)
15. 1975 DPOY CB PIT (3,6)
16. Raiders center 1960-1974, 1st ballot HOF (3,4)
18. SB X MVP, PIT, Lynn (5)
19. Trevor Lawrence college (7)
21. HC (4,5)
23. A player who fails to meet expectations of drafting team (4)
24. Drafted 1st overall in 2020, LSU (3,6)
25. Synonym of "snap" (4)
26. Signed a 114 million dollar contract with Miami in 2015, previously DET (9,3)

Down

1. Beat CHI in Super Bowl XLI (5)
3. Cowboys CB, Trevon (5)
4. Intercepted pass at the goal line in Super Bowl XLIX (7,6)
5. Beat Washington in Super Bowl VII (5,8)
7. Replaced Phil Simms on CBS (4,4)
10. Browns RB, Kareem (4)
11. QB drafted 3rd overall in 2021, 49ers (4,5)
12. Beat DEN in Super Bowl XLVIII (7,8)
14. A five-yard foul which occurs when the offensive team does not put the ball in play before the play clock runs out (5,2,4)
17. Peyton Manning college (9)
20. SB XLVIII MVP, SEA, Malcolm (5)
22. Round Terrell Davis was drafted (5)
23. Any position not typically aligned on the line of scrimmage (4)

Puzzle #43

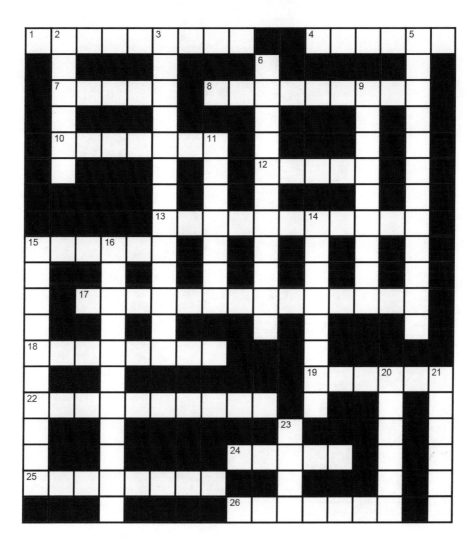

Across

1. RB nicknamed "Juice" (2,7)
4. Worth 2 points (6)
7. Bengals franchise INT record holder, Ken (5)
8. 1978 DPOY LB DEN Randy (9)
10. Cardinals (7)
12. Bills 85-99, HOF, Bruce (5)
13. 2020 DPOY LAR (5,6)
15. SB IV MVP, KC, Len (6)
17. Browns coach since 2020 (5,9)
18. Tom Brady college (8)
19. Texans owner, last name (6)
22. Most career postseason INTs, 49ers, HOF (6,4)
24. A defensive maneuver (5)
25. Buccaneers division (3,5)
26. Deshaun Watson college (7)

Down

2. Cowboys LB, Lee Roy (6)
3. SB XLI MVP, IND (6,7)
5. SB XXXII MVP, DEN RB (7,5)
6. Butt Fumble (4,7)
9. Lines between which the ball begins each play (4,5)
11. Falcons RB, 2000+ rushing yards single season, William _____ (7)
14. Kyler Murray college (8)
15. 2X Pro Bowl RB, Muscle Hamster (4,6)
16. Dolphins owner (7,4)
20. Bo Jackson college (6)
21. SB XXVI MVP, WASH, Mark (6)
23. This play is part of the triple option strategy (4)

Puzzle #44

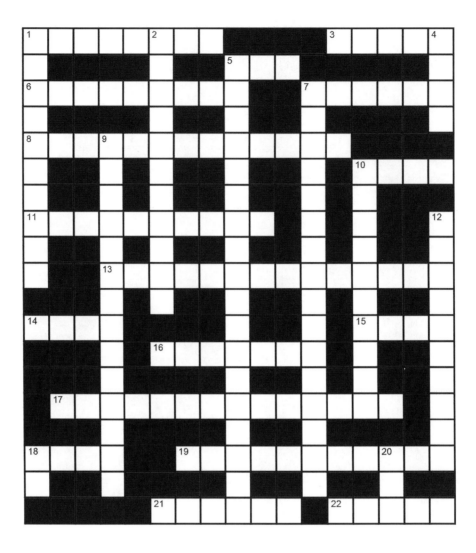

Across
1. 1971 MVP MIN (4,4)
3. SB XXX MVP, DAL, Larry (5)
5. Point after touchdown (3)
6. 49ers ownership family (9)
7. Houston (6)
8. 1st player to throw for 400 yds, 4 td passes, and 50 rushing yds in a game, HOU (7,6)
10. A weighted yellow cloth thrown by a field official (4)
11. Saints gadget QB (6,4)
13. Giants/Jets stadium (7,7)
14. Troy Aikman left FOX for this network (4)
15. Troy Aikman college (4)
16. In 1988 they moved from St Louis to ____ (7)
17. 2005 MVP SEA (5,9)
18. Middle linebacker in a 4-3 formation (4)
19. Rams HOF DE who coined the term "sack" (6,5)
21. An on-field meeting of team members (6)
22. Indianapolis (5)

Down
1. Red Rifle (4,6)
2. Falcons coach since 2021 (6,5)
4. ____ tackle; tackle in a three-man defensive line who lines up opposite the center (4)
5. Madden 10 cover, PIT Troy ____ , ARI Larry ____ (8,10)
7. Time warning at end of game (3-6,7)
9. WR with long last name, TJ (14)
10. The official traditionally in charge of timekeeping (5,5)
12. Washington (10)
18. Also known as jack; interior lineback, 3-4 formation (2)
20. National Football League (3)

1

2

3

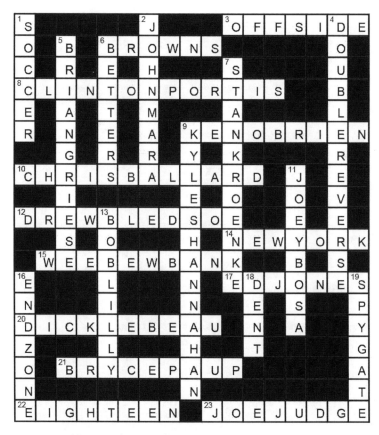

4

5

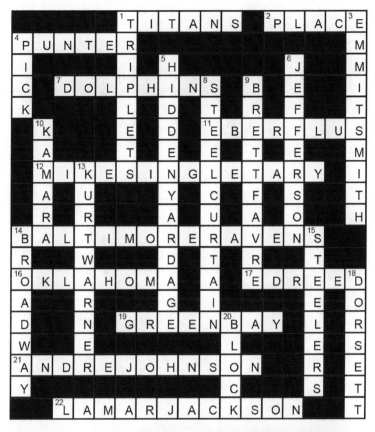

6

7

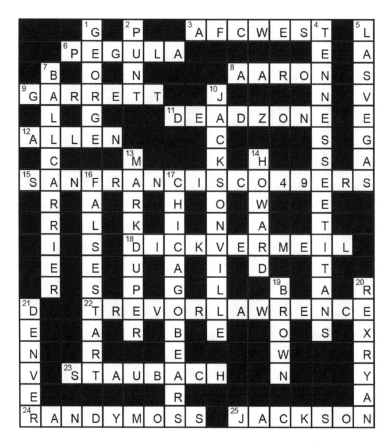

8

9

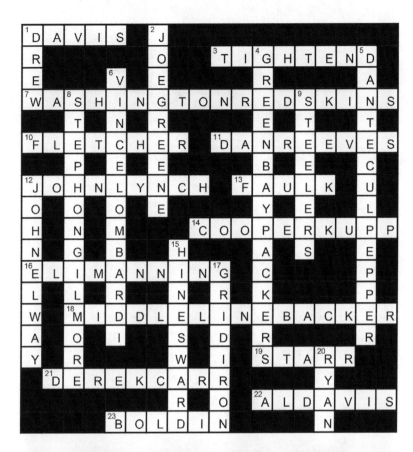

10

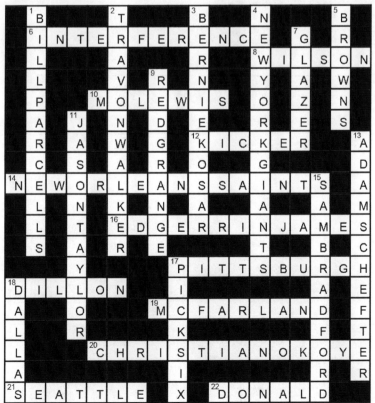

11

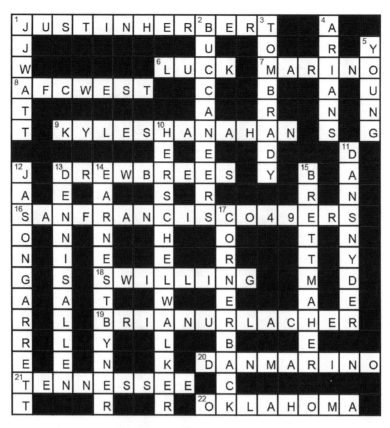

12

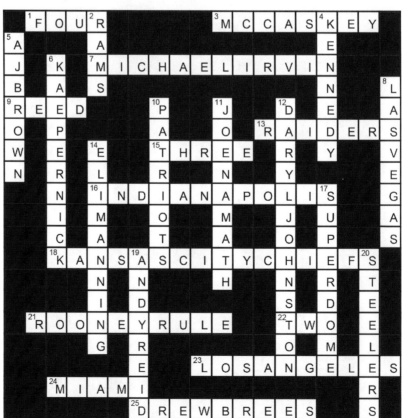

13

14

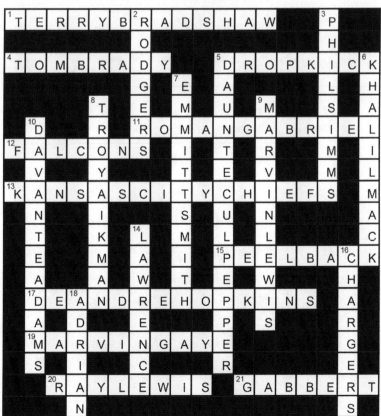

15

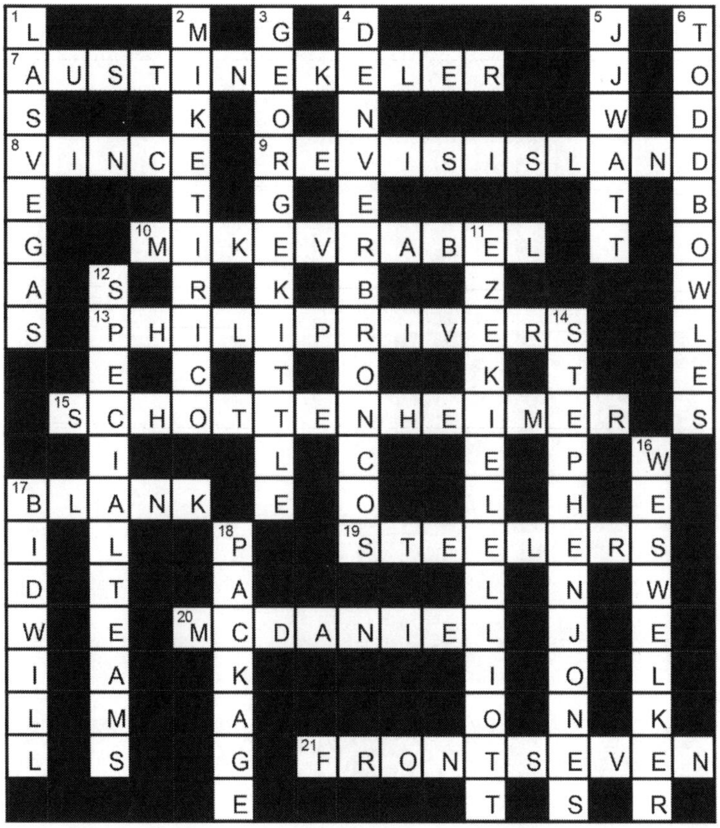

Across:
- 7. AUSTINEKELER
- 8. VINCE
- 9. REVISISLAND
- 10. MIKEVRABEL
- 13. PHILIPRIVERS
- 15. SCHOTTENHEIMER
- 17. BLANK
- 19. STEELERS
- 20. MCDANIEL
- 21. FRONTSEVEN

Down:
- 1. LASVEGAS
- 2. MKONETG
- 3. GONGECTO
- 4. DNECOLHONTS
- 5. JJWTT
- 6. TODDBOWLES
- 11. LZKTPHONK
- 12. SRKBZ
- 14. STKTRPSWELKR
- 16. WESWELKER
- 18. PAGE

16

Across:
- 1. PETERSON
- 5. OKLAHOMA
- 6. PANCAKE
- 9. STUBBLEFIELD
- 11. CHASEYOUNG
- 12. HOUSTONOILERS
- 15. WILLIAMS
- 17. MATTRHULE
- 20. FITZGERALD
- 21. MATTRYAN

Down:
- 1. POWARNER
- 2. CEVEERE
- 3. JHNNRINNE
- 4. DANIEREED
- 7. KAANN
- 8. JAAKS
- 10. BBRGGINNE
- 13. RSASS
- 14. PUN
- 15. WIDERS
- 16. MOSLEE
- 18. TITIFES
- 19. PAYATTO

17

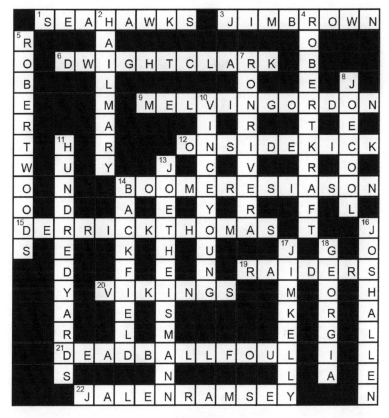

18

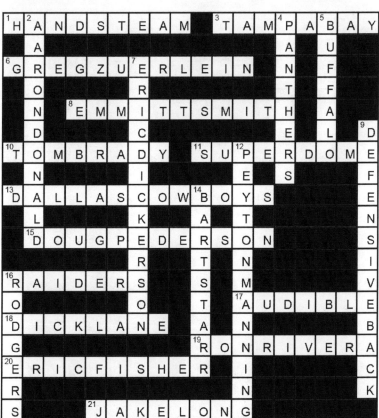

19

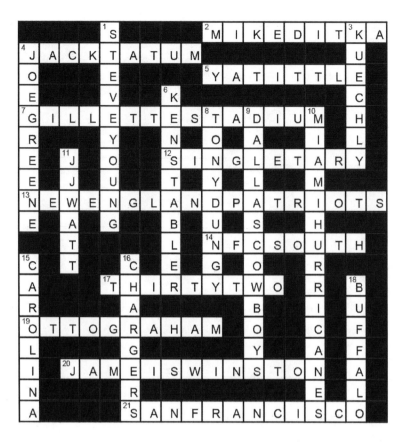

20

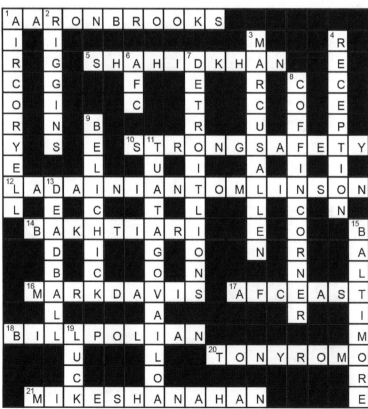

21

22

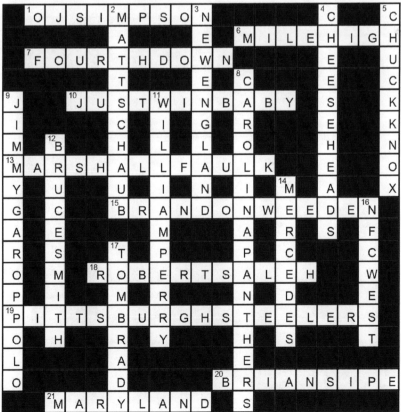

23

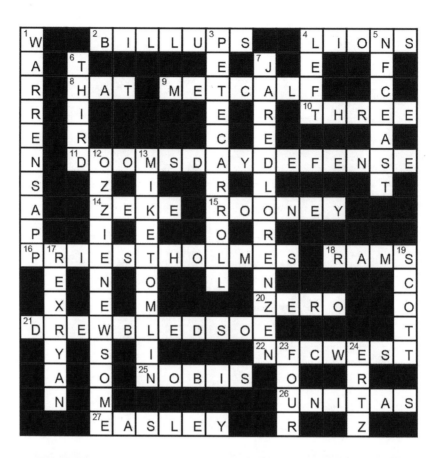

24

25

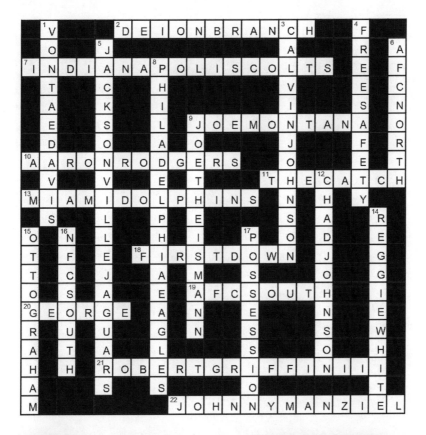

26

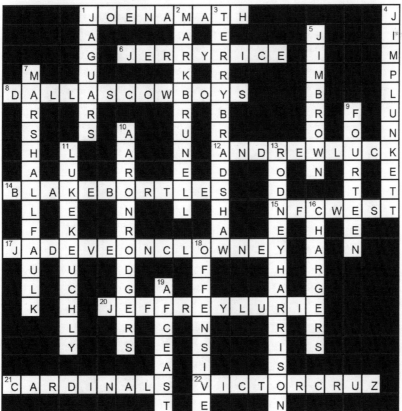

27

28

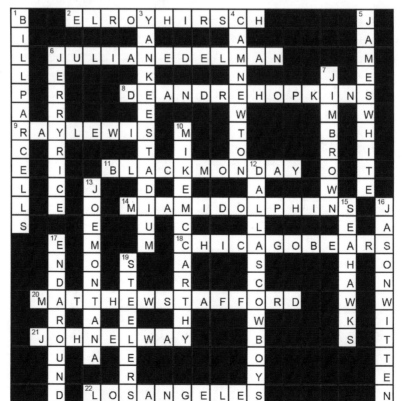

29

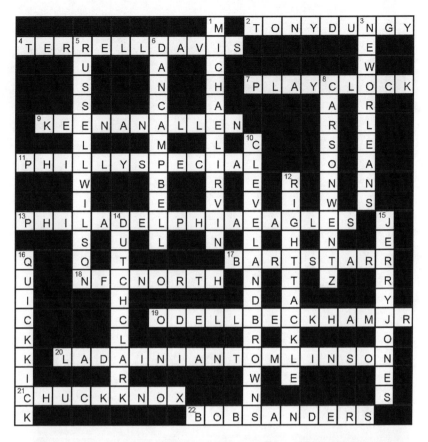

30

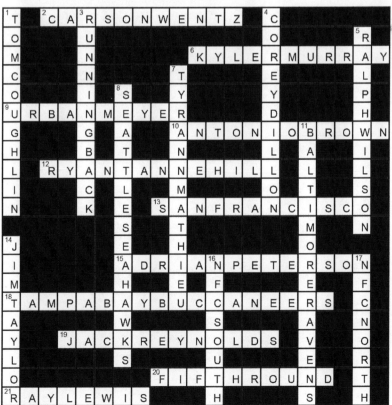

31

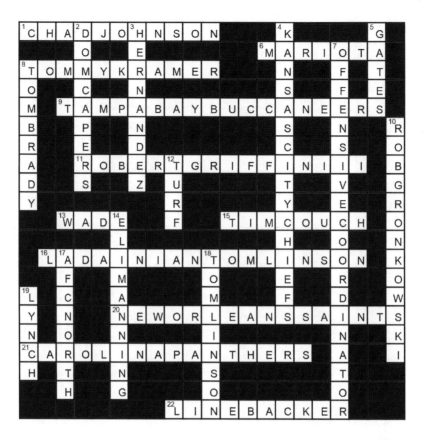

32

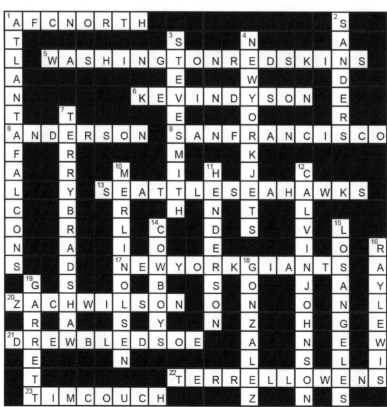

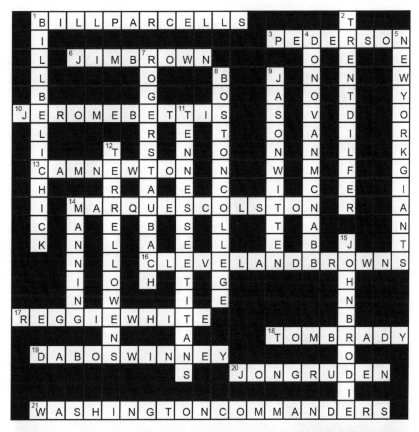

35

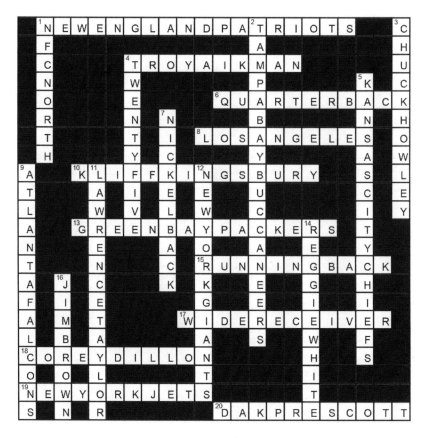

36

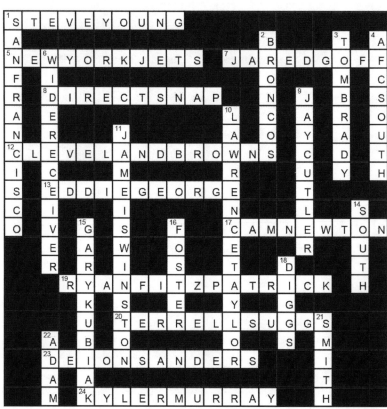

39

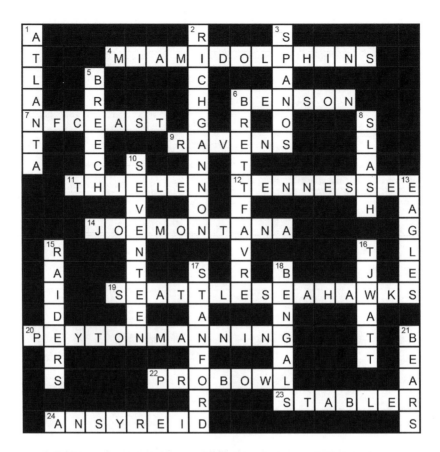

40

41

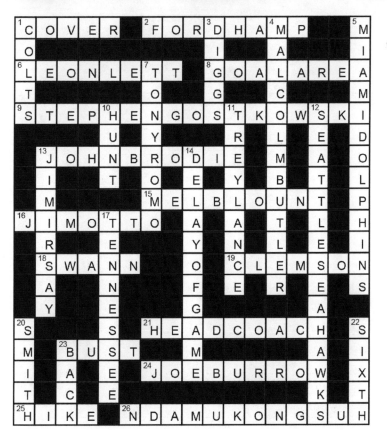

42

43

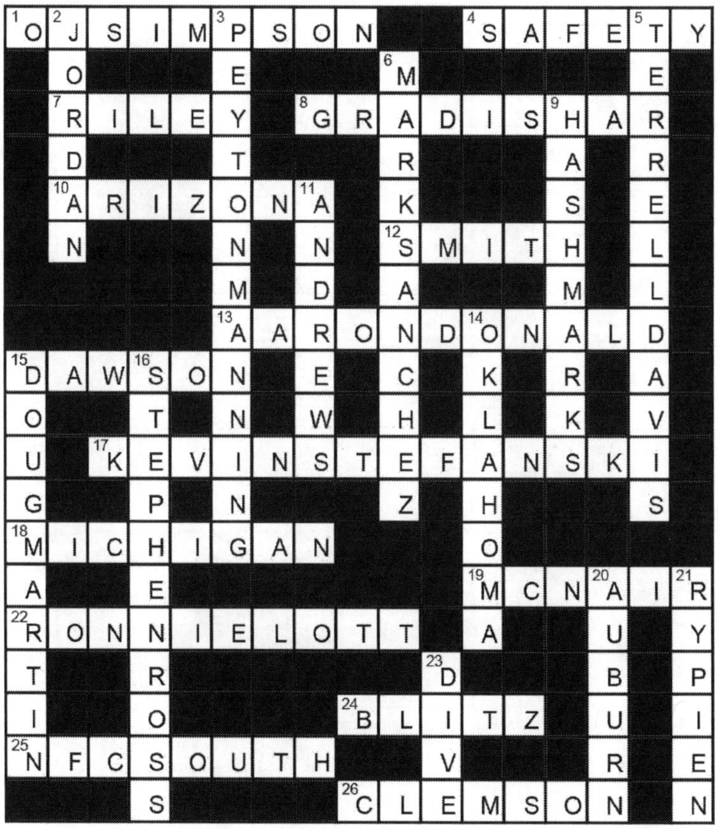

Across and filled grid:

- 1: OJSIMPSON
- 4: SAFETY
- 7: RILEY
- 8: GRADISHAR
- 10: ARIZONA
- 12: SMITH
- 13: AARONDONALD
- 15: DAWSON
- 17: KEVINSTEFANSKI
- 18: MICHIGAN
- 19: MCNAIR
- 22: RONNIELOTT
- 24: BLITZ
- 25: NFCSOUTH
- 26: CLEMSON

Down entries visible: JOE, MET, MARK, HARASSELL, ANN, ANMD, STONPNE, KEPN, DOUGMATIA, RTRO, DBUV, NS, CS, RYPIEN, etc.

44

- 1: ALANPAGE
- 3: BROWN
- 5: PAT
- 6: DEBARTOLO
- 7: TEXANS
- 8: DESHAUNWATSON
- 10: FLAG
- 11: TAYSOMHILL
- 13: METLIFESTADIUM
- 14: ESPN
- 15: UCLA
- 16: ARIZONA
- 17: SHAUNALEXANDER
- 18: MIKE
- 19: DEACONJONES
- 21: HUDDLE
- 22: COLTS

Made in the USA
Las Vegas, NV
18 December 2024

14625310R00039